For

Happy Reading

Jim Walters
16/12/08.

THE VICEROYS:

SO NEAR YET SO FAR

BY JIM WATTERS

with Barry Gordon

978-1-4092-3380-0

First Published 2008

TABLE OF CONTENTS

ACKNOWLEDGEMENTS

Firstly, I'd like to thank my mother and father for all the support they have given me throughout my life; my kids, Kevin and Sarah, and their mother, Anne.

I'd also like to thank all the lovely guest-house owners who were so kind and helpful to the band over the years: Phyllis Lynott (Manchester); Nettie Stewart (Leeds); Mrs. Ahern (Ibrox, Glasgow); The Paris Hotel (Highbury, London).

Of course, The Viceroys' fans, especially those in the Dumfries & Galloway, and Wigtownshire region.

Albert Bonici, the Italian promoter who looked after us so well – and so often – during many tours of the Scottish highlands.

And, finally, a special thank-you to Barry and Shona.

FOREWORD
by Barry Gordon

"Jim Watters? No, sorry, never heard of him."

That's what I said, when one of my editors contacted me one sunny afternoon in August 2007. Apparently some chap, who used to perform with an Irish showband during the '60s and '70s, wanted to write a book about his life in the band - and would I be interested in helping him write it?

"What was the name of his band again?" I quizzed my editor. "The Viceroys you say? Sounds like a reggae band from Jamaica to me. Well, I guess I could go and meet up with him and see what he has to say."

So off I went.

When I first met Jim he was standing outside the famous Glasgow Barrowlands Ballroom. A stocky, bespectacled man with a flame of red hair sticking out from underneath his Gecko-imprinted hat, I asked Jim if he was actually Van Morrison instead. We've been laughing and joking ever since. In the year-and-a-half following our first initial meeting, I've come to know Jim a great deal: a real, down-to-earth, salt-of-the-earth man. Over the many hours we've chatted in various

Glasgow pubs, clubs and coffee houses, it's been a real education to learn about the essence of what showbands were all about. The suits, the choreography, the ability to tailor one's performances to a particular audience, the musicianship - you can almost smell the Starch and Brasso within these pages.

From Jim's early days growing up in Drogheda, to long, lazy summers in Sligo listening to folk music in his grandparents' kitchen; from his involvement in the Irish showband music scene to the trials and tribulations faced along the way, Jim never seemed to lose his loving belief in the sacred qualities of a life dedicated to music.

Now there's even talk that Jim and the rest of The Viceroys might reunite in the wake of this book. Will it happen? All I can say is I am looking forward to help pen the follow up. Enjoy.

THE SECOND COMING

"There you go, Dad," my son said. "Recognise this?"

Kevin climbed into the car and handed me a photograph. It was Easter Sunday in Glasgow and I had driven round to my son's flat to take him to mass. I stared hard at the photograph in my hand. To say I was stunned was an understatement.

"Where the hell did you get this?" I replied, bewildered. "I never knew this even existed."

It was a picture of my old band - The Viceroys. Earlier in the week my teenage daughter, Sarah, informed me that Kevin had found some photographs of my old band on the Internet search engine, Google (the younger generation's answer for everything these days). I was concentrating on driving her to school at the time so barely noticed what she said. Imagine my surprise, then, when Kevin presented me with The Viceroys' first publicity still, taken on a staircase in a hotel in my hometown of Drogheda in the Irish Republic back in 1965.

I studied the photograph like a monk studying a page from the Bible. There we were: the first incarnation of The Viceroys: immaculately dressed in sharp-looking suits, wearing toothpaste-white smiles and perfectly sculpted Brylcreemed hair. Young and naive, I stood on the far right of the picture, unmistakable by my fuzzy red hair, Buddy Holly-style glasses and cheeky Irish smile.

"Are you telling me you got this from off the Internet?" I asked Kevin, holding up this long-forgotten snippet of showband memorabilia.

"Sure I did," Kevin said, smiling back at me. "Face it, Dad, you're famous at last."

He was right. Almost three decades after The Viceroys had stopped playing gigs, and after all the years we had slogged it out trying to make a name for ourselves, we had finally become known to millions of people around the world at the touch of a button - and I didn't even know about it!

On the drive home after mass, I contemplated the symbolism of discovering this piece of my past on Easter Sunday, the day of Jesus' resurrection. Was Kevin's discovery a coincidence or was it meant to be? Perhaps it was a sign; a sign that would lead to another resurrection - the Second Coming of The Viceroys. I felt like I was experiencing a revelation. What happened to The Viceroys I wondered? How did the band come to an end? What became of us all? Was there a chance we could all get back together again?

Just like in the Blues Brothers movie, I felt an overwhelming urge to embark on my own "Mission from God." It was time to "get the band back together."

At first I could barely remember anything about what we had done. It was all so long ago. Everything seemed so... hazy. Then it all started to come back to me. There was only one thing to do. It was time to get the telephone book out.

A VISIT

When I went round to Jim Delaney's house he was nowhere to be found. I hadn't seen him in a long, long time. Probably about ten to fifteen years. His garden lawn was spirit-level flat, the hedges neatly pruned, but the windows of his two-storey detached house were all blackened out, big bags of rubbish left lying out beside the front gate.

It was November 2007 and I was back in Drogheda for a short visit. One quiet afternoon I went to visit Jim, who was in no doubt the most talented member of The Viceroys. A Jerry Lee Lewis-look-alike who sported a big, black, curly toupee, Jim Delaney could play the guitar (as Chuck Berry once sang) like he was ringing a bell. He could also play saxophone and piano with dazzling ability. It didn't matter whether it was Elvis Presley, Hank Williams, Frank Sinatra or Ludwig Beethoven - Jim could play anything you asked him. He was a good man, too, and a good laugh.

When he joined the original line-up of The Viceroys on bass-guitar (somewhat ironic given his sensational talent on the sax and piano), in 1965, I was thrilled. It was like having Hank Marvin in your band.

Unlike the rest of the band, though, Jim was a lot older than us. He gained a lot of sympathy, as well as our respect, because of his very noticeable stutter. Nevertheless we were in total awe of his playing ability. He could play with one hand tied behind his back, and often made orchestrated hand signals during performances, shouting out what notes to play whilst playing at the same time. Sincerely, he was that good.

Jim, however, was what you might call a homebody. He never liked touring, and if he could get back home to his own bed after a show he often would. Needless to say his time in The Viceroys was all too brief; as the band took on more gigs away from home, Jim eventually handed in his notice. I was sad to see such a huge talent leave the band, but there were no hard feelings between us. I just hoped he would go on to be a success locally.

When I eventually caught up with Jim at his house a couple of days later, I was shocked at what I saw before me. A few years earlier, Jim had been earning a good living playing piano in one of the local hotels. Unfortunately, attendance had started to drop when new owners took over the hotel. Staff had to be trimmed down, and, unfortunately, Jim was one of them to be shown the door.

Around the same time, his sister, who he was very close to, and who did pretty much everything for him, passed away. Jim, the poor soul, went to pieces. He stayed indoors more often than before, rarely venturing out for nothing more than a newspaper or a pint of milk. Just before his sister died he bought her a gigantic flat-screen television. Now he was stuck with it, and spent the majority of his day sat in front of it watching whatever junk was on. Worse, as his mood began to deteriorate, he went down to the local music shop and did the most self-destructive thing he could have ever done - sell all his musical instruments. This was crazy. Jim lived and breathed music. It just wasn't right. It just wasn't Jim.

As I sat down on a tatty chair in Jim's living room listening to all of this devastating news over a cup of tea, it was clear my surprising visit had caught him cold and unprepared. He was very depressed and withdrawn. Holes littered his shirt, almost threadbare due to the amount of times it had been washed. His baldness was now covered by a baseball cap instead of a wig. There was food stains on his trousers and burn marks on his jacket.

As we talked, Jim revealed that he could no longer play a musical instrument. His badly affected confidence and deep-rooted depression had caused him to develop a psychological inability to perform.

"I can't put my fingers on the keys anymore," said Jim, resigned. "I can no longer play any music at all."

I felt a lump in my throat. How could it all come to this? What a waste of a great talent.

"Jim," I said softly. "I'm putting a book together - about my time with The Viceroys."

I mentioned it tentatively, hoping Jim's mood might brighten at the mention of the band.

"Who knows what may come of it. Maybe we could all meet up one day? A reunion if you like?"

Jim used to be defensive at the best of times. Now his shutters were well and truly pulled down.

"What, Jimmy?" he remonstrated. "You mean go back out in the wagon and go touring again? I, I, I can't do that."

Jim had begun to stutter now. He always stuttered badly when he got nervous. I felt terrible; vexed I ever brought the subject up.

"Those days are over for me now, Jimmy," he went on. "I am too old and unwell for that kind of thing."

I squirmed uncomfortably in my chair, feeling somehow partly responsible for Jim's physical and mental demise. Undeterred, I tried to focus on the good times.

"Please don't fret, Jim," I told him, "am not too worried about the band side of things just now. I'm more interested in getting some stories. You know, for the book. You were always pretty good at telling stories. Can you remember any?"

Jim paused, as if gathering his thoughts. A minute passed, which felt like forever. Then, suddenly, he piped up a little.

"Well, I do seem to remember a gig we played at the Beachroom Ballroom in Aberdeen. Yes, the Aberdonians."

A small smile began to form on his weary face.

"They were a strange audience, weren't they, Jimmy? They all just stood staring at us in stony silence - stiff as tin soldiers. It was as if they had looked straight into the eyes of Medusa. I thought we were going to get bombed out because we weren't playing music they liked. I thought we would get lynched."

I was heartened by Jim's response, delighted to see he was finally making an effort with me.

"They threw pennies at us during that gig," Jim continued. "I thought they hated us but it was just their way of showing us they actually appreciated our performance. Then we played a gig not long after, somewhere in the highlands, where the audience wanted heavy metal and we were giving them folk music instead - The Clancy Brothers and The Dubliners and the like. Aye, that was funny."

As we talked some more about the band I was surprised to learn of a secret Jim and Brendan (The Viceroys' first singer) had kept away from me during their time in the band. Brendan was a hardy drinker, and, as it turns out, Jim was subbing him money in order to fund Brendan's drinking while we were away on tour. I was a little bit shocked as I was oblivious to it at the time. However, I was relieved to learn Brendan always paid Jim back, and it was clear Jim was fond of Brendan, whom he said was a good professional with good musical etiquette. He would always praise Brendan's singing, going so far as to compliment him on being able to reach a high C - one of the hardest notes to reach - on Gene Pitney classic, I'm Going to Be Strong. It was a tune we often tried hard to "make a fist of" (a phrase we used for knocking a song into shape during rehearsals), but Brendan's vocal had done it a justice.

In return for helping Brendan fund his drinking, Jim made him promise to attend mass one Sunday morning after a Saturday night gig we had in Elgin. Brendan agreed - he just had no idea it meant getting up at 6am.

"Mind that, Jimmy, eh?" laughed Jim. "Brendan was so hung-over he turned up to mass wearing a huge jacket to disguise his beetroot-purple face. He was shaking from his hangover so badly he looked like a big piece of raspberry jelly. That was hysterical."

We'd been talking for three-quarters of an hour when Jim went all quiet again, suddenly announcing he had to go outside and tend to something. I wasn't sure if it was an excuse to end my visit but I just smiled and thanked him for taking the time to chat to me. Closing the front gate behind me I paused, turned around to look at Jim's house again and let out a long, heavy sigh. I felt terrible seeing Jim in the state he was in. He was a musical hero of mine and he could have gone on to be one of the true greats in music. If only I, The Viceroy, had made a visit to him earlier, maybe then I could have saved him. One thing was for sure, though: if I was going to get the band back together it was going to be much harder than I thought.

RISE AND EDUCATION

I was baptised James Henry Watters (Jimmy to my pals) in the mid-'40s. My parents, who came from Sligo in the west of Ireland, moved to Drogheda on the east coast of the country to work at one of the local weaving factories after training in Northern Ireland - where I was born.

My mother was an honest, kind woman who worked in a factory with 300 other women, and I vividly remember our house was always full of cards and ornaments from fellow employees who'd sent gifts, as tokens from their holiday jaunts around Europe and America.

My father on the other hand, played traditional music and hated rock and pop music. He was a fiddle player, and often on school holidays I'd visit my relatives in Sligo: a strong area for traditional Irish music my great-uncle called "down home". At lunchtime, or, long after the pub had closed, their friends would regularly turn up at the house for tunes, often playing in my granny's kitchen. None of them could read music; they were all natural, "feel" players. To get a tune going, they would simply whistle the first few bars, and then the other fiddlers and accordionists would join in.

My grandfather, Patrick Watters, lived until he was 94-years-old, and was always flush. He had fought for Independence, as a member of the Irish Republican Army at the beginning of the 20th century, and whenever I used to visit him he'd often give me a fiver, which was a lot of money in the '50s. I felt bad about taking the money from him until my mother pointed out he had three different pensions: an old age pension, one from the Irish Republican Army, and a police pension (my grandfather was also a Bobby). What was he like, eh?

My granny meanwhile, was also a musician and a highly regarded accordion player. She used to set up what they called "Dancing Boards" situated at crossroads in the rural areas outside Sligo, where people from four different directions would all meet up and play music. Most people in today's society wouldn't believe such events ever took place, but they did, and they were my first memories of music during many lazy summers in Sligo.

Drogheda, though, is my hometown, and where I would spend the majority of my young life. A small town with a population of around 30,000 situated on the east coast of the Irish Republic, Drogheda was one of the walled towns that Oliver Cromwell - a controversial 17th century English military and political leader - attempted to seize control of. The river that runs alongside the town was used as part of the town's defences. One of the main gates, complete with a drawbridge and a gantry at the top, still stands there today. It's very Robin Hood, don't you think? I certainly thought so when I was a wee boy growing up there.

Drogheda, however, is also the site of an infamous massacre of the Royalist defenders: The Battle of the Boyne, which occurred near the town at the River Boyne in 1690.

On a more positive note, Drogheda was a very big weaving town producing everything from towels and linen to tapestry for bedspreads. The town produced shoes for big shoe companies, oil for Stork margarine, and has a big cement factory that sends concrete all around the world. Coca-Cola has a factory there, too, and subsidised a lot of the things in the town, even providing a free bus service for the townsfolk. A former member of The Viceroys now works for an American syringe company in the town, as well.

When I was growing up, downtown Drogheda was all full of Teddy Boys in blue suede shoes. All the rock 'n' rollers wore drainpipe trousers, teenagers hung out in coffee bars drinking milkshakes and listening to the latest chart hits on the jukebox, and there was always a fight at the weekend, often involving chains and knives. For a kid, though, it was quite a safe town and not unlike any other small town in the world. Everyone knew everyone else - not even James Bond could get through town undetected - and I would often cycle to school every day. There were no cars or buses to take you there and back, so if you didn't have a bike, you were staring a fifteen-minute walk in the face no matter if it was rain, hail, sleet or snow. Nevertheless, I enjoyed riding my bike, and I always used to stop off at the bus station on my way to school on a Monday morning to see all the showbands return home from their weekends away playing music. I sometimes wondered if I might become part of a showband myself. The whole lifestyle seemed exciting to me. But then a lot of things do when you're a kid.

At school I longed to be a pilot - I still want to be a pilot! I thought about it seriously, and worked out how to get into the Irish Air Corps, which, basically, consisted of three Vulcan bombers, a few Cessnas, and a couple of Spitfires.

Subject-wise, Geography and English were my strongest - I'd often be teased by my future band mates for being such a swot at school - and all looked to be going well. That was until one day the nurse came round to give all the school pupils the standard eye test examination. Struggling badly just to read the first three lines on the eye-test board, the nurse put it very succinctly when she said: "Why aren't you wearing glasses, Watters?"

My pilot career was over before it could even begin. I was only 14. The whole event reminded me of a tale my mother used to tell me, about how the owner of the local opticians was such a good salesman, even if you sent a cat down there it wouldn't leave the shop without a pair of glasses on its face. I was to be that next cat.

Like every other school in the '50s, discipline was high on the agenda amongst strap-happy teachers. We had one Brother who used to slag us all off, often addressing us as "Ye of the valley of the squinting windows". To those outside Ireland, this was a colloquial term for a society obsessed with providing neighbours and peers with a good perception of one's own personal matters. In other words, he thought we were nosey little gossipers. He may well have been right. He came from Kerry, in the south of Ireland, which is where all the big footballers came from. He was also very, very strict. He often had me up at the blackboard by the locks of my red hair, banging my head off it: "See that, Watters!?" he'd scream at me. "Do you understand!?"

Then he would kick you under the desk if you hadn't done your homework. You wouldn't get away with that kind of thing nowadays. He was also quite fond of giving us the cane.

Tom Murphy - these days a big shot with Air Lingus in administration - was a sly kind of boy. He'd always have something plotted. He would often bring in a razor blade and slit the edges of the teacher's cane - which stood at the edge of his desk - all nice and cleanly. So when the Brother came in and discovered we hadn't done our homework he'd line us up for the cane. Unsurprisingly, the cane would splinter when the first lad got smacked, much to the Brother's fury, and our amusement.

The Brother would say: "Aye, Murphy, I bet that was you that did that," staring straight at him like a hawk spying a field mouse.

The Brother would then take some money from out of his pocket and send someone down town to fetch him another cane. The ploy, then, was to have the lad who got sent out to fetch the new cane well-schooled. As we had a forty-five minute class, his job was to delay as long as possible, so when he returned there wouldn't be enough time for the Brother to give us all a good lashing.

"Lad, what took you so long?" the Brother would bark on his eventual return.

"Sir, the first shop was all out of stock, so I had to go to another place," the lad replied shaking with fear.

"Well, seeing as it's nearly the end of the class," the Brother said, "I'll let you little rogues off with it just this once. But you've all been warned."

We all breathed a collective sigh of relief. We'd got away with it... just.

Music, on the other hand, was my first love, and I must have been about 12 or 13-years-old when I first took an active interest in it. Summer days in Sligo listening to my relatives playing traditional music had inspired me, so when my pal told me he was going to the Crilley School of Music to study accordion, I decided to join him.

The music school was basically a normal house with a big room and a garage off to the side. It could accommodate 15 people when there needed to be music stands and a piano set up - but only by opening a big door that connected the big room with the garage.

For my parents, going to the school meant buying me an accordion, a chromatic button accordion with 80 bass buttons. In the '50s this type of accordion cost approximately £300, an extraordinary amount of money. Nowadays, they cost about £3000, so I was very grateful that my parents financed the accordion to get me started in music.

Miss Crilley, whom the school was named after, was my teacher. A spinster in her mid-40s, she wore old-fashioned dress: tweed skirt down to her ankles, thick tights, flat shoes, and her hair tied up in a bun. She was a no-nonsense mistress who taught me to play chromatic accordion, which, I felt, was a mistake. Why? Well, on my accordion - a chromatic accordion - each button produces two notes: one when squeezing the bellows in, and one when pulling the bellows out. On a piano accordion, however, the keys produce only one tone whether the bellows is being squeezed or pulled. This meant those who learned how to play piano accordion could play a regular piano, whereas I, who had studied the chromatic accordion and who had always wanted to play piano, would have to take up normal piano lessons instead.

The ages of the pupils ranged anywhere from 5 to 17-years-of-age, and the school was not too dissimilar to that of a factory production line: new, utterly interchangeable students replacing the old ones who had grown up, graduated and left. By the time it came for me to represent the Crilley School of Music at competitions, I was a big, fully grown man (well, almost).

One such competition was the Irish National Competition, in Limerick, where we entered as a ceilidh band in the ceilidh section. We had a drummer and double-bassist but our teacher, Miss Crilley, had to rely on volunteers to play the other instruments due to the unavailability of other musicians. On the day of the competition our drummer couldn't get the day off work, so I had to (no pun intended) fill in for him. The competition was also judged in a bizarre fashion. One of the judicators gave you marks for daft things - looking like you were enjoying yourself being one of them. He'd say: "These young people look like they're enjoying themselves - they're tapping their feet and smiling."

There was another, second school of thought that implied if you were a good musician then you shouldn't be tapping your feet at all. Nevertheless, I sat there smiling, playing away contentedly. All we had to do was play an old time waltz rhythm, a 4/4 fox-trot and perhaps a march or a reel. Fortunately I could keep time pretty well, so neither dragged the band back nor steamed ahead. Given the problems we had, I was surprised we finished second overall.

A more painful experience, however, was endured when we went to Dublin to do a radio broadcast, which was usually a half hour slot. Sometimes you could be landed with playing the children's hour at 5pm in the afternoon, or at 10pm at night. We got the evening slot. So there we were, The Crilley School of Music Band, and we're outside the studio getting the equipment out the van, when, accidentally, I let the hatch fall down, thus crushing my fingers. Ouch! I let out a high-pitched, bloodcurdling scream that would have deafened a dog. I was in total agony, hopping up and down the pavement like a madman. The rest of the band must have thought I'd invented some new dance craze. I ran into the studio's kitchen and put my swiftly swelling hand under the water tap but it did little to alleviate the pain. When it came time for us to play - an announcer would come on beforehand to say a little about the band first - I was still writhing in pain, my hand tucked firmly under my arm, like I was pretending to be some injured war soldier. Even so, I was determined not to let the band down, so I did the best I could, pressing down on the accordion keys as lightly as possible so not to cause any further injury to my bulbous hand. Thankfully the band were on fine form and covered for me brilliantly, therefore any bum notes I made - and there were quite a few - went virtually unnoticed.

Afterward, as was the want in those days, we usually went to the cinema, then off to a dance before heading home: a day away in Dublin was a great opportunity to get away from the parents. However, it was practically impossible to enjoy myself with my hand causing me so much discomfort, and when I got back home that night I couldn't sleep a wink. The pain was driving me mad.

Next morning - Sunday morning - I headed off to chapel, my hand now covered in a bandage I'd badly applied myself. It throbbed so violently my hand felt like one giant pulse. Halfway through the sermon I got up out of my seat, headed towards the door and stumbled outside, certain I was going to pass out. Being a man - stubborn in other words - the last thing you would do was go to a doctor if you had an ailment. The hospital, however, was only ten minutes up the street and the pain was now excruciating. It felt as if I had toothache in my hand. So off I went.

When I arrived at the hospital, the doctor - a nun - took off my bandage and stared hard at the big green and yellow pulsating balloon that had taken the place of my hand.

"Right!" said the Sister. "You'll need a tetanus injection in the bum for that. Your finger is so badly infected, had you left it for another hour or so it would have had to be amputated."

Amputated!? I could barely believe what I was hearing. My face must have turned whiter than the hospital bed sheets. As it transpired, when the hatch had fallen on my hand it had pushed the nail right underneath the skin of my finger causing a giant, yellow-coloured, almost-lose-your-finger infection. Rarely have I felt such relief than when the swelling went down later that evening.

At 14-years-of-age, I had missed out on the opportunity to train as a pilot due to bad eye sight. Now, three years later, I'd almost lost a finger. Which just goes to show: had I not left the church any sooner than I did, I would not have had any musical career at all. Luck? I'd prefer to call it divine intervention.

THE ROYAL VICEROYS

During my final year at the Crilley School of Music, I also had a quartet on the go. Just two accordions, drums and guitar, every Sunday we played a tea dance inside a local school hall. It gave us some extra pocket money; some much-needed experience, paid for the furnishing of our own instruments, and helped hone our chops.

After that year was over, I, and the rest of us at the Crilley School of Music went our separate ways. One went on to become a dentist, the other an accountant (each to their own, I suppose). At just 18-years-of-age, one of the quartet's members - the other accordionist aside from me, and one of the most talented musicians in all of Ireland - surprised us all by jacking in music in order to join the Priesthood.

Eamonn Campbell, meanwhile, who also played in the quartet, would later go on to play tenor banjo in the world famous Celtic folk band, The Dubliners. So at least one of us became famous! Campbell was a terrific solo guitar player and could easily have worked with the likes of The Shadows or alongside Duane Eddy.

For me, though, music had simply become a pastime - a hobby if you like. Instinctively, I reckoned I'd always wanted to be in a band; to play in front of big, appreciative audiences, and go on tour. Rock 'n' Roll was a fever and I, like any other teenager, was equally excited and inspired by it. With the experience I had gained from The Crilley School of Music, I figured I could make a few bob from music. I was never going to achieve my ambition as a pilot, and I had spent so many years studying my art I decided I may as well try and make it as a musician.

Not long after I had made my decision to become a musician, Frank Zappa released an album called Lumpy Gravy - a reference to the fact that what most musicians ate was brown and very lumpy. How right he was. Being part of a four-piece band, I swiftly realised I would need to add a few more instruments to create a more dynamic, more appealing group.

When we started the touring band we would often be standing on stage with an accordion. In the early '60s, pop groups didn't have accordion players in their line-up. Sure, in today's pop world it's widely accepted, but back then, if you were playing fiddle or accordion in a pop band you were laughed at - that was old granddad-type stuff.

Trombone, on the other hand, was regarded as a cool sounding instrument. The pop songs of the time (Bend Me Shake Me, Everlasting Love, etc.) all had sax, trombone and other brass instruments in them. So did a lot of The Beatles' material. It was the in-thing. Then, soul music came along. Anything the Stax soul label put out I lapped up with all the voraciousness of a hungry dog. My mind was made up. It was time to put down the accordion and pick up the trombone.

Trombone was new to me, though, and with a new band formed and ready to hit the road, I had to learn quickly. Luckily, soul songs all relied on long, sustained notes: fixed positions on the slide. Listen to Knock on Wood and you'll see what I mean. You wouldn't have to play a solo unless you were playing Dixieland or jazz, and our new sax player would show me where to hold the slider to get notes like B-flat or F-sharp. You had to purse your lips instead of blowing straight in to get one note, then, purse them higher and tighter to get the next note in the same position. It was difficult at first but it was something that had to be done.

We wanted to get the band going.

We also needed a name.

During the '50s and '60s, artists like Wayne Fontana and Dave Berry had names for their own backing bands; things like The Searchers, The Seekers, or The Tremeloes for example. On top of this, all the showbands of the day had names like The Highwaymen, The Platters, and The Miamis. We had to find a name just like that, only different. Names like these are a world away from the names bands are giving themselves today. Funeral For A Friend? My Dying Bride? Dogs Die In Hot Cars? Whatever next - Scratch My Bum? Whatever, it wouldn't surprise me.

Anyway, Robin Hood and King Arthur was what captured my imagination as a kid, especially as Drogheda had huge 16th century defence walls, and big drawbridges with moats. So when I formed the new band I was intrigued to learn that Mount Baton was the Viceroy of India. The Viceroys title had been originally used in the Aragonese Crown since the 14th Century for Sardinia and Corsica, royal officials who govern a country or province in the name of the monarch. It might have been a strange name to give a bunch of Paddies; nevertheless I thought we could represent the people of Ireland in the same way.

Medieval knights and the Sheriff of Nottingham fired my inventiveness, too, so when the time came to create our band's logo I designed a King Arthur-style shield with a big, Sir Lancelot-type sword running through it. I was only a young man at the time when I had to think up all of this but no-one ever questioned it. It wasn't a case of "You'll have to change the name of the band before I come and play with you." It was more like: "So what's the name of the band? The Viceroys? OK, fine." It must have been acceptable to the rest of the lads for no-one ever queried it.

Over time, I also drafted in another guitar player, as well as a keyboard player and a sax player. We were amateur - some of us had day jobs - and our short tours away to England simply weren't enough to pay our way. It was tough enough just getting the time off work to play. Worse, we were not just competing with other showbands, but major recording artists as well.

Sometimes we'd land a good gig down in the likes of Killarney, in the south of Ireland, but it was 250 miles away. There were no motorways in those days down there, no dual carriageways where you could get the butt end of the journey completed in a couple of hours whilst cruising at a steady 80mph.

Even Donegal, another good gig, was a three-and-a-half hour journey away from Drogheda. That was fine, if you were Elvis and had the Lisa-Marie, or Led Zeppelin with their Starship - a forty-seat plane that had a bar, Thomas organ, kitchen, television, artificial fireplace, a den, and a fur-covered bed built into it.

And yet, while the President of the United States could jet around in Air Force One, we, however, had the Beetle to get around in. It only had two extra seats in the back, which doesn't leave much space - or ventilation - when you've got loads of gear to pack in. The Beetle could go on forever but it couldn't pull the wings off a butterfly, and always took an age to get us anywhere.

We played 30 gigs in a row travelling in the Beetle one time, often over single-track roads, and even had to change its engine nine times one night just to get us to a show. When we reached 100,000 miles on the clock, I asked everyone in the back of the wagon to raise a cheer. But its time was soon spent. Eventually my mother insisted that I "bite the bullet" and buy a proper wagon fit enough to carry us around the country. So I bought a Commer van. I was afraid the payments would be too big to handle but it turned out to be one of our best investments.

Fortunately, we only went through three wagons during The Viceroys' career. Without a good van we'd have had no career at all, and it's with hand-on-heart I can honestly say I never injured anyone whilst driving it, nor did I cause any crashes.

The only scrape I can think of, came during a gig in Liverpool when I drove through the Mersey tunnel and had my wing mirror clipped.

Saying that, we almost had a big accident on the M6 once just outside Manchester. I could see a big flow of Smith & Maddison trucks coming in the opposite direction. They had these tiny, neon signs on the side of their cabs. It was 6am, so, to alleviate the boredom I began counting them. I got to about fifty or sixty when all of a sudden I heard the word "Jimmy!" screamed down my ear. I was heading straight for the back of a tipper truck that was right in front of me. I had been driving at 60mph while the tipper was cruising at a steady 50mph. Had our guitarist, Ronnie, not snapped me out of my hypnotised state we would have most likely ploughed straight into the back of the tipper truck. It was a close call. And thankfully the closest I'd ever come to a major crash. Or was it?

A little closer to home, our early gigs of 1965 and 1966 involved playing all kinds of different shows. Like playing Miss Rosebud shows for instance. These types of concerts were essentially beauty pageants held within a ballroom: good-looking, very well-dressed girls dancing the night away hoping one of the judges would pick them out for being the most presentable, best dressed or what have you. These kinds of things are frowned upon in the 21st century, but in the swinging '60s they were the norm. All we had to do was play swings and waltzes to keep everyone dancing.

We also used to arrange what is called a Hop - a meeting place for young people to listen to live music and dance. We'd hire out the basement of the local town hall, make up our own posters and notify the local colleges so we could make sure loads of girls would come to the gig. We'd attract well over 200 people to these gigs, sell lemonade and ginger beer to make money, have a raffle, and then we'd belt out the pop tunes of the day.

Eamonn, who went onto play with The Dubliners, often played solo numbers like Walk Don't Run or We Have All The Time In The World. It was basically a get-together for teenagers, an opportunity for them to get away from their parents.

The money we were earning wasn't exactly what you might call a King's ransom, either. We all had day jobs to pay our way as amateurs, and it wasn't unlike me to play the occasional wedding. In fact, there was one Saturday night early in The Viceroys' career where I had to play three weddings in a day. It was one of those freak occurrences where all three bands booked to play the weddings had either pulled out, had mysteriously fallen ill, or simply couldn't be bothered turning up to play the gig.

So there I was, playing a show in the afternoon, another show at teatime, then another one at 8pm. I literally had to skip from one hotel to the next. Making up an excuse wasn't easy. All I could say was: "Look, I've done my two hours, now I have to go." It was a horrible thing to do and I never wanted to let anyone down. All I'd do was play some old time waltzes, a wee bit of ceilidh, some quicksteps, fox-trots, jigs and reels.

In the '60s, people didn't mind if it was just an accordion player who provided the entertainment; now, though, in the modern day, it's only discos people want to hear. Just look at funerals now: even they have entertainment, and usually in the form of some wailing, female singer. Worse, they bring a full-sized PA into the church with them. Soon as someone cranks up the PA you're ready for the stone to fall from the church roof. If I'd known people were willing to pay £200 for someone to sing at a funeral in the '60s The Viceroys might just have cornered that market, too.

The truth of it, though, was showbusiness was tough. Thankfully, my parents always encouraged me, but they were naturally worried about me being away from home quite often; not because I might get into trouble, but because I always seemed to be driving all the time. And driving + tired, poorly-paid musician = potential crash on the road.

Once I drove straight from London all the way to John O' Groats whilst maintaining my managerial duties of arranging gigs and organising accommodation on the drive up (I had to stop off at various service stations to make the necessary telephone calls). I was pretty sure that James Brown, the so-called hardest working man in showbusiness, didn't have to do his own driving, lug his own gear around or make his own packed lunches. If he did, he'd probably call it "paying your dues." I'd paid plenty.

My first year cutting it as a musician was meager on the wages front all right. You wondered where your next gig was coming from, it was a chore keeping up with learning the new hit songs of the day (no Internet or CDs back then to help you) and getting the right amount of sleep was virtually impossible.

All of a sudden I was counting my change, trying to work out how to make a bag of pasta last, and how many miles we could go to the gallon. Even the guitarists were keeping the strings on the necks of their guitars a lot longer than they used to. Maybe it was time to postpone the music malarkey for a little while and get a real job? God, help me, I thought.

GET A JOB

I had been looking to subsidise my low-budget musical career for a couple of weeks when one day, not long out of bed, I looked out the living room window and spotted a Christian Brother coming down the street on his bicycle. He stopped outside my house, jumped off his bike, and walked up the path and chapped on the front door. So I went out to meet him.

"How are you doing this morning, Brother?" I said, outstretching my hand to shake his.

"Good morning Master Watters," he replied, "I was wondering - have you found any day work to supplement your music-playing career yet?"

"No, Brother Kilkenny, I haven't," I said.

"Well, Master Watters, it's your lucky day. I have a job for you."

I made a loud gulping sound in my throat, the sort you hear on cartoons where the unwitting victim realises something particularly unpleasant is in store for him. Oh God, I said to myself, eyes planted heavenward. What's this going to entail exactly. "I want you to go up to Saint Patrick's school, there's a job for you there. You start at 9am on Monday morning. OK?"

And that was it. A Brother chaps on my door when I've barely put a spoonful of Cornflakes down my gob, and he wants me to go back to school? I'd only just left the place for heaven's sake.

"Why, a job at the school, Brother? Why, that would be... great." I tried to keep the bemusement on my face to a minimum.

"I take it I'd be doing some cleaning and some other form of janitorial work?"

"Oh-no, nothing like that," said the Brother, climbing back onto his bike. "You'll be teaching."

"Teaching?! I can't do that, Brother. I don't have any qualifications for a start."

"Nonsense. You've taken your A-levels, haven't you?" said Brother Kilkenny. "You've had a good secondary education. Am I right?"

"Well, I suppose," I replied sheepishly. "But what do I know about teaching a class?"

"Come on now, Watters, lad," the Brother implored, pedalling away from the gate slowly. "You're a young man with a good education. Surely you can teach 7 and 8-year-olds how to read and write, do their sums and whatever. Just get up to the school on Monday. Cheerio."

And with that he was gone.

Five days later, I was standing in front of a class of forty primary school kids about to give my first teaching lesson. And not just any class, either. This was the headmaster's class! Christ almighty! I was nervous as hell. In fact, I felt more nervous than I usually do five minutes before going onstage in front of a big crowd. All the kids in class sat and glared at me as I shuffled my way into the classroom, staring at me like I had ten heads or something. Who the hell is this guy, they must all have thought.

Struggling to comprehend the fact I was now a teacher, the first thing I was meant to do was call out the Registrar. Fair enough. That's pretty easy. Then, of course, they began to test me out. One by one, they'd start chatting, and then another one, and then another one - before you knew it there was a classroom full of tiny terrors screaming the house down. When I eventually restored some order, I decided to do something relatively simple by reading them a story, but it was no use. One of them, a kid named Thornton, stood up and looked me straight in the eye.

"Will you please sit down, Thornton," I said. We're all trying to learn here."

Casual as you like, his response was swift and to the point. "Fuck-off!" he shouted.

Well. I had no idea which way to look, what colour to turn, or what to do. This was an 8-year-old upstart telling me to eff-off. I was mortified. I came from a generation where if you said something like that to your teacher you didn't get a second go at it: you got the bloody belt. But this was a national corporation school.

"I'm not taking this from you pal," I snarled at the little punk. "You sit down right now and shut your mouth - now - or else!"

So he sat down. Then another pupil piped up and he started giving me jip, too.

"I'm bringing my father up to you," he spat.

"Well, am sorry son," I retorted, "I'm just trying to do a job here. But if that's the way you feel, fine."

This was too much. I'd rather have continued my life as a starving musician than face this band of little beggars each day.

Then one other lad - who constantly stood up, and who continually ignored my instructions to sit down - walked over to the window and stared out towards the flower bed in the gardens where the bees were gathering nectar from the blooming flowers. He was totally absorbed with it. What I didn't know was that he was a remedial with learning difficulties. What really annoyed me, though, was no-one had told me about him; no-one had warned me or informed me of his special needs. And here I was giving him a hard time now. What a carry on. But the stress didn't stop there. Oh no.

Later on that evening I went down to the local shop to buy some groceries, when three of the boys who were giving me a hard time earlier that day met me outside the shop. Here we go, I thought: trouble outside the classroom. This was all I needed.

"How you doing, Mr. Watters?" one of them, Thornton, I think, said, nice-as-nine-pence.

"Aye, I'm fine. Thanks for asking."

"We'll see you in the morning, then, Mr. Watters?"
"Yes, of course," I smiled back at them. "I look forward to it."

From that moment on they were all fine with me. It took a wee while to get used to them all, right enough, but I never got any serious grief thereafter. I reckon they were just testing me out, to see how far they could push the boundaries.

Unfortunately, what was meant to be a three-week teaching stint, turned out to be a whole seven months when it was revealed to me the headmaster would be laid up for longer due to lung problems and the onset of pneumonia.

After just one month teaching, my nerves were shot to bits. I'd taken on one or two gigs with the band, but when I saw my first month's pay packet I nearly had a stroke. I couldn't believe how much money teachers earned compared to performing musicians. Better yet, you had a full hour for lunch, morning and afternoon breaks, plus you could leave at 3.30pm. That gave me more time to rehearse with the band. We were still a quartet, still semipro and still doing occasional gigs in Donegal, often returning home late on a Sunday evening. It left me exhausted for teaching the next morning, but on one of those Sunday evenings I was to receive some tragic news.

It was midnight and I had just arrived home after driving a 200-mile-radius to a gig in Northern Ireland. My mother, who was still up when I arrived, was sitting in the kitchen with an expression on her face that needed no words to convey her feeling.

"Your grandfather has just died," she said softly.

Now I was young at the time, about 17, and I didn't really know how to react or know what to say when those kind of things happened. I just stared at her with sympathetic eyes.

"When is the funeral?" I muttered. It was all I could think of to say.

"We'll have to go now, James. Immediately," my mother said. "Are you able to drive?"

My grandfather lived on the west coast of Ireland, more than a few hours drive away.

"Of course, not a problem, mum," I said.

In truth, I was overtired and desperate for sleep. However, in such circumstances, you'll do almost anything... no matter how bad you feel.

As we set off, the roads were as white as a sheet. Just like a glass bottle. I was shaking, not just because I was nervous of the driving conditions, but also because I was tired and hungry. My father couldn't take my mother as he had to open up the factory in the morning. He just couldn't up sticks and go like that, so I had to take her. I thought back to when I was 14 and driving my grandfather's tractors in the rolling fields of Sligo: I was always a good driver.

Thirty miles short of Sligo, we got to the Corlewe Mountains, a small mountain range. We were halfway up it when snow came pelting down on top of us, the car skidding all over the place. I didn't have that much experience of driving in those sorts of conditions at the time and was worried there would be another two dead people on their way to heaven. Thankfully we got there safely, at around 4am in the morning.

When we arrived at my grandfather's house all my other relatives were holding a sort of wake for him. It was at that moment - seeing all the musicians in my family come together in the same kitchen they always used to have tunes in - that I had another one of my Revelations: I had to make a go of forging a career in music. It was time to quit the teaching gig. It was good timing anyhow, as the headmaster of the school had returned to the school in good health. I was only a substitute teacher, and as there was no vacancy there or elsewhere, my teaching days were at an end.

I left with as much fanfare as when I began. I was idle then for a few months; desperation had crept in; I was writing away for interviews and nothing was coming back. Then I spotted a job advertised in Dublin at AEI Hotpoint Appliances - white goods basically. I got an interview and when I turned up I realised it was a store-man's job I'd applied for. The manager, who was interviewing me, looked over my application: "Mr. Watters, it appears to me you're overqualified for this job. Tell me, why exactly did you apply for it?"

My reply was a simple one.

"I'm broke for one thing. I've been sitting in my house going crazy for months now," I said, plainly. "I want to work. Please, sir, I need a job."

"But this job is in Dublin, son, you know that? You'll have to travel from Drogheda every day. Are you really willing to do that?"

"I'll be taking the train," I impatiently informed him. "My only problem is I won't be able to get in for 9am in the morning. The train arrives into Dublin on the north side of town, so by the time I hop on a bus to the south, where the factory is, I'll be late."

"OK, then," said the manager. "Do you want to start at 9.30am, then?"

I was hired.

After the interview was over the manager had another word with me about my education, promising to offer me a better job at the plant should I show enough willingness in the role I'd just been hired for. So we shook hands. It was a deal. Now in a new job, I got to meet the foreman, who, in-between his persistent effing and blinding, organised all the deliveries around the city. When I was a young man starting out, computers were not as common in the workplace as they are today, so he used to mark off all the stock as the invoices were brought to him with a stock-card. Sometimes there were special deliveries, like to big events for example, and I'd often be sent along to make sure none of the stock got damaged.

The managing director at the time, it must be said, certainly thought a lot of himself. He drove a Jaguar, wore a camel-skin jacket and had a personal secretary, who wore a miniskirt, legs all the way up to her earrings. He was known as PM Walsh. He came into the office one day and shouted: "Is Jim Watters free?"

If PM asked, PM got.

"Come into my office, Jim" he said, ushering me in. "We've got a problem here. We've got three appliances that we can't locate - all left-handed, cream-coloured fridges - and I'd like to get to the bottom of it. I don't know who's at it, but the van driver has been trying to find them and he's had no luck. Perhaps he can't be arsed to look for them properly. Now, the foreman downstairs assures me the cards have been marked and that they've gone out, but the driver has them marked on his notes as having not been delivered. I don't know where they are! So, anyway, Jim, I want you to go down to Dublin Docks and see if you can find them. Is that understood?"

So off I went.

I spent five hours with the van driver crawling about the Dublin Docks warehouse. The warehouse also belonged to Kellogg's as well as Hotpoint, and I proceeded to get covered in dust (I was wearing trousers and a shirt), as I ventured up ladders, tight-roped it across metal beams, all the while trying not to kill myself by falling 50 feet off warehouse shelves in the process. There was certainly no sign of any damn cream, left-handed fridges anywhere. This was ridiculous.

On my return to the plant, the sales manager wasn't in a good mood.

"Now, Jim, are you absolutely sure you didn't see what we're looking for down there? You have been down there, haven't you? Well what did you do?"

I was frustrated and annoyed by his pedantic attitude.

"Look, I turned all the cartons round, checked all the labels, climbed up over every last box and still couldn't find them. Are you happy now?"

"Jim," he said, putting his arm around my shoulder, lowering his voice to speak. "There's a lot of bother going on all over this. Would you please go back down to Dublin Docks tomorrow again and double check?"

I was adamant.

"Please, I can assure you I've covered every square inch of that warehouse and they're not there. But if it'll make you happy, then I'll go. You can ask the drivers, they're witness to it. I've checked everywhere."

So, next day, down to the warehouse, and there I am covered in stoor again. I returned back to HQ and told the sales manager precisely this: "I swear on my mother's eternal soul there is nothing there. We've checked everything ten times over."

He still wasn't happy. With three machines missing and an irate foreman who swore (literally and often) that he hadn't booked them out, he was defiant they were still in stock. So where the hell were they?

Meanwhile, there was a sales manager in the sales office I had been promoted to, who said we hadn't been meeting our targets and that head office in London were complaining that sales were down. That meant he had to go back on the road to sell while I was left at his desk to do all the calculating and invoicing.

Unfortunately, Clive Sinclair hadn't invented his calculator by that time so I had to use a book calculator instead, which wasn't exactly fun to count important figures on. It was like being back at school again.

A week passed when a salesman from Kilkenny came up one day to our office to meet the boss. As the disappearance of the cream-coloured, left-handed fridges was the talk of the store, I asked him if he had heard all about it.

"Oh aye," he said. "There's been a helluva hullabaloo about the whole thing from what I've heard. But I think I might be able to shed some light on the whole thing, Jim. Leave it with me and I'll get back to you."

Sure enough, the following week the salesman from Kilkenny is back on the phone to me. He told me he'd been doing some detective work and discovered that three appliances had been sent out to a hotel for a trade show. From cookers to electric fires and fridges - one of everything had been sent out, including an invoice for two cream-coloured, left-handed fridges. I looked up the invoice from the name and address the salesman had given me, and yes, two cream-coloured, left-handed fridges had been loaned out without being charged for it. Turns out they had been sent to another trade show - this time in Limerick. Finally, we had found two of the machines. But there was still one left unaccounted for.

A month passed and everyone had but given up the ghost on finding the missing machine. Gradually it became forgotten about completely.

Towards the end of my time at the factory - there's only so many 40-hour weeks of selling household appliances you can take - myself and the rest of the staff were invited up to PM's house for a party. He had invited all the major companies and distributors to his house - a plush pad in Dalkey (Bono of U2 has a house there today) that looks over onto Kiliney Bay. It was a big wine party and all the heads of the electricity boards were there. With plenty food and booze around it seemed churlish not to indulge. As everyone mingled, the sales manager and I stepped into PM's kitchen to grab a beer from PM's left-handed, cream-coloured fridge.

"You playing any gigs again soon, Jim?" said the sales manager, a wry smile strewn across his and my face, alike.

"Sooner than you think," I replied, closing the fridge door for him. "But only if I can find a sax player. You know any?"

BLACK MAGIC PAT

"Hi, I'm Pat," said the little guy outstretching his hand to shake mine. "I hear you need a sax player - am one of the best around. When do we start gigging?"

"Tomorrow," I replied. "You're hired."

The Viceroys were about to embark on a Scottish tour that would take us all the way across the north-east of Scotland: from Tain to Kinross, from Huntly to Morayshire, from Keith to Aberdeen. Bookings had started to come in thick and fast prior to my leaving Hotpoint and I was keen to take on as many gigs as possible. Trouble was the band needed a new sax player.

Our regular saxophonist, Billy, had to remain in Ireland to take care of some personal family matters, so, I, as manager, had no choice but to put up advertisements in the Musicians Wanted section of the local newspaper. We could have played without a sax in the line-up, but in a showband you need at least six people in the band: any less than six in the group and you were called a pop band. Besides, the audiences, as well as ourselves, loved the sound of sax, and we felt self-conscious about standing onstage with only two-thirds of a brass section. Fortunately for us, a fantastic sax player named Pat - no-one knew his surname - turned up at my mother's house one day dressed in a dark crimson suit, his sax tucked neatly underneath his arm.

Now, The Viceroys had undergone many changes of personnel during its life-span. It was like a revolving door sometimes; a bit like Spinal Tap and drummers you might say. We probably had more line-up changes than we had rehearsals, but that was the nature of running a showband. If someone was unavailable for whatever reason, you got somebody else in who could do the job quick-smart. So, with the entire band packed into the wagon along with all our gear, we set off for Lossiemouth in the Scottish highlands - one of our favourite places to play.

Pat had no problems integrating with the rest of the lads in the band, he was an easy-going sort. Always smiling and never short of a word for himself, what we didn't know before the tour was that, Pat was into Black Magic. He told the rest of the band he only flirted with it, bringing it up in conversation as casually as one might suggest sticking the kettle on for a cup of tea. There were many hours and many white lines to eat up on the road, so it wasn't exactly unusual to talk about a broad array of subjects, even topics surrounding the metaphysical and the afterlife.

The band were curiously intrigued by Pat's ability to wax lyrical on the subject, and on the way up to the highlands we agreed (with reluctance on my part) to hold a séance back at our digs in Elgin after the gig in Lossiemouth.

In the '60s, Lossiemouth was a training centre for British navy pilots, the Harriers. It was also the height of the Troubles in Ireland (1968), so when a van full of Paddies arrived at the security gate we thought we'd get some serious jip from the officers. There was about as much chance breaking into Fort Knox with a toothpick than getting past such British military establishments. Thankfully, all we received was some serious belly-laughs with the officers. They were glad to see us, and glad to be getting the entertainment. No mirrors under the van for us I'm glad to say. When we did get inside the camp we found ourselves sharing the bill with Zoot Money's band with Andy Summers (who would later go on to achieve mega stardom with The Police) on guitar. Zoot's band were a big draw at the time, they had a big hit in the charts with Big Time Operator, and carried a huge Hammond organ around with them in a trailer just so Zoot could play it whenever he felt like it. As we unloaded our gear, the servicemen told us that if we were quick we could get into the canteen and have as much grub as we wanted. We were starving musicians for Christ's sake - so in we went, on the double. And what a big spread it was, too: beans, potatoes, bacon, eggs - the lot.

This particular show, however, was what they called a pajama ball, where all the men had to wear nighties and wigs. The women, on the other hand, wore slinky pajamas, which was pretty sexy if you ask me. All in all, it made for a great night.

Afterward, back at the digs, we were all very excited and nervous, as we sat round a big glass coffee table waiting for Pat to give us our first experience with the paranormal. Pat laid out the letters of the alphabet before inviting everyone in the band to place their fingers on the top of an empty tumbler.

"Now as we're all amateurs here, lads," said Pat, "we're not going to go into the heavy Black Magic right away. OK?"

Everyone nodded in agreement. The question now was: who do we contact? Jesus? Wolfetone? Deceased family relatives? No. Marilyn Monroe.

Within a few seconds of the séance it was clear we hadn't contacted Norma Jean but a vicious spirit instead. The tumbler started shook violently. Not just moving about the table uncontrollably, but moving under the table as well! We all clocked each other, eyes wider than a rabbit staring down the headlights of an 18-Wheeler truck.

"I think we've contacted a bad spirit," said Pat, as if butter would melt in his mouth.

"No shit!" said Joe, the bass player, speaking on behalf of all of us.

Now we were getting every piece of foul language thinkable spelt back at us, every obscenity under the sun. It was disconcerting to say the least.

"Has anyone got any Rosary beads?" said Pat trying to keep his cool.

Faster than Speedy Gonzales, our pint-sized guitar player, Ronnie, produced a large string of Rosary Beads from his inside jacket pocket and put them on the table. Pat put down a crucifix.

"The test here," said Pat "is for the spirit to knock the beads and the crucifix off the table. If it does, we're all in big trouble."

Great, that's all we needed to hear, I thought - a wee, simple challenge for our unfriendly demonic spirit.

The tumbler crept to the edge of the table and again shook violently but the Rosary Beads stood firm. You could feel everyone in the room relax a little. Suddenly the tumbler shot all the way back down the table before stopping short of the Rosary Beads again. Some of us needed to make a quick trip to the toilet. Fast. The tumbler resembled a children's spinning top, fizzing away under some sinister supernatural force. Then it stopped dead as a Dodo. Everyone froze. I felt a sudden need to vomit. The goodness of the Rosary Beads had stopped the bad spirit from... well... I didn't want to think about what it might have brought about. At this point, though, you'd think we'd forget the whole bloody thing and, pardon the pun, get the hell out of there. But, oh-no, Pat insisted we continue, as he didn't want to leave a bad spirit inside the house.

Later on, we contacted some dead comedians who spelt out some rather good jokes. It was going not too badly by this point, then, all of a sudden the windows flew wide open, the curtains almost blowing off their hooks. The lights started to flicker. One of the lads, I think it was the trumpet player, started shouting "Jesus, Mary and Joseph - protect us - we're all going to be damned!" He was in a right panic; he was shitting himself. The rest of us just laughed, albeit nervously. Well, what could you do? The trumpet player took it very, very badly. Then the makeshift Ouija board spelt out two messages that would have a big impact on our psyche for a long time to come.

The first message said: "You're going to have a big problem at the weekend. When you get to Glasgow, there's going to be lots of people there - they're not going to be happy."

Sure enough, we did have a gig in Glasgow that weekend. But what did it mean?

Then, another worrying message: "Jimmy. Phone Mama. DTE. Urgent."

Now what the Hell did *that* mean? Some of us were seriously freaked, me especially. It was squeaky bum time. As the rest of the band tried to figure out what the spirit meant about our gig in Glasgow, I began fretting terribly over what DTE meant. Sick with worry, I phoned my mother immediately after the séance but I couldn't get through to her. In those days, you had to go through an intercom operator, and you couldn't reverse the charges, either. I hoped and prayed to God that no harm had - or would - come to her.

The very next day I still couldn't get through to my mother. In fact, it wasn't until the following day she finally answered the telephone, much to my relief. She told me of a promoter from Portadown, in Northern Ireland, who wanted to know, as soon as possible, whether or not The Viceroys could play St. Patrick's night - the biggest-paying gig of the year. At least that shone some light on the possible "urgency" of what the Ouija Board was describing. I told my mother to ring the promoter back and tell him we'd do the gig. But what the hell did DTE stand for?

Throughout that next week the rest of the band started receiving "messages". They began writing down obscure, pseudo-meaningful pieces of information, they believed, was being sent to them from a higher power. Every road sign, every news-stand headline, every word from every page in a book they turned to, they believed to be communication from another dimension. Now life on the road can drive you crazy, but this was overstepping the mark, Twilight Zone stuff. It was getting scary.

My personal belief is that we, as humans, all have a kind of power within our own minds. After all, we only know about 0.009% of what the brain is capable of. I mean, who thought that one day we would be able to send messages through the air? And who is to say that in years to come we might be able to send information, cranium to cranium, without any electronics involved at all? So when I continued to hear about the band receiving these messages - though I believed in the possibilities of it - I also believed it wasn't something we should be tampering with. So I went and looked for Pat.

I told him it had gone too far. All the gobbledygook, all the brainwashing, his influence was proving deconstructive, shit-hot sax player or not. So I pulled him into a coffee bar for a little chat:

"Pat," I said. "Come on now. Put an end to all of this, eh? You're being controlled by all this Black Magic mumbo jumbo, it's just not healthy. One day, you're going to wake up and your man with the horns is going to be at the bottom of your bed."

I was certain I had scared him, because the next day all talk of séances and black magic stopped. Everyone decided we weren't going to dabble in that kind of thing anymore. It was finished. And not another peep was said about it again from that minute onward.

Later that year, I called up a girl who worked in the local telephone exchange. I got to know her and her friends due to the hundreds of calls I made on behalf of the band. One night, I went down to the flat where her and her friends were staying. I asked one of them – a lovely girl named Helen - about the message I received during the séance in Elgin, and enquired as to whether or not she knew what the letters DTE stood for. Helen, fairly new to the job, just shook her head. Margaret, her flatmate, however, and who had been working at the telecom for more than five years, finally shed some light on the whole thing.

"I know what it means," she told me. "DTE is an old telecom term that is rarely used anymore - it means Distance Trucks Engaged. In other words, you can't connect your call to whomever you want to."

That was it? That was what DTE meant? The reason I couldn't get in touch with my mother that evening - the lines were engaged. Who could have foretold that? Even if Pat was on the wind-up, which I am sure he wasn't, not even he would have been privy to that sort of information, surely. The Ouija board must have been telling the truth.

By this point though, Pat had left The Viceroys. He served on just one tour before Billy returned to the fold. We never heard of Pat again, that was, until we saw the Irish-Italian's name in a London newspaper a year later.

Apparently he'd landed a new gig with a showband who had a residency in North London. Most strange of all was that the newspaper article finally shed the light on what Pat's surname was. At last we knew: De Ville.

A PRAYER ANSWERED

Pat had forewarned us about dabbling in the spirit world when he was in the band. Now it had backfired on us spectacularly in the form of bad karma. For when we got to the Irish Club in Glasgow we finally discovered what the Ouija board meant about our "big problem at the weekend".

When we turned up to our gig on the Sunday night there were not one, not two, but three wagons sitting outside – we had been triple booked! We didn't get to play and we only received a third of the money we were due for the night. As was the case with some promoters, this particular one wasn't for putting his hand in his pocket and honouring his commitment despite his error. So his card was marked. We didn't have enough money to afford digs, so we set off for Stranraer where we would get the ferry back to Ireland.

Tired and hungry - the promoter ensured we weren't fed - we stopped off at a hamburger stall usually reserved for working taxi drivers, and one of few places you could get something to eat in the wee small hours in the '60s.

Naturally, being the designated driver, everyone managed to get some sleep apart from me. Nevertheless it gave me time to think - mope more like - about how short of money I was. As the band were on a weekly wage, I had to pay the band, leaving yours truly with, well... not very much at all. I sighed and wished to the heavens that we would find another gig the next night before having to sail back to Ireland. Of course, the next night was a Monday - the most difficult night of the week to land a gig.

Nevertheless, we arrived at Stranraer first thing in the morning confident there would be no problem getting aboard the boat with all our gear, which was the size of a small-boat itself. Wrong. Because it was summertime, scores of holidaymakers had booked up all the space there was months in advance. You could be standing there for four-to-five days and still not get back to Ireland. The shipping company was very sympathetic though, and did try to get us back across the water. Bands were coming and going between Ireland and Scotland all the time; they valued our custom, especially during the winter, however there was no space for us on the morning crossing so we had to wait until the evening; which meant having to hang around Stranraer all day.

By about 4pm that afternoon I returned to the ferry terminal to fetch a bag from the wagon when one of the office staff came and found me. Apparently someone had telephoned the office and wanted to talk to me. Me? How would anyone have known I was at the ferry port? Bemused, I walked up to the office and took the call.

"Hello," I said, tentatively. "This is Jim Watters speaking. Uh, how can I help you?"

Ten minutes later we were back on the road, heading towards Newton Stewart and in high spirits. Only three things we on our mind now: girls, a few pints of beer, and something hot and tasty to eat. We were going to make a right evening of Monday night. There was nothing surer.

The person on the other end of the phone was one Mrs. Laurie. She ran a club in Newton Stewart, not too far from Stranraer, and was desperate for a showband to play that night as part of the annual gala. The band she had originally booked, another Irish lot, had phoned to say they couldn't make it. In other words, the buggers - who were touring England - couldn't be bothered coming to Scotland, so returned home to Ireland via Liverpool instead. With bands forever going back and fore between Scotland and Ireland there was always a chance a band would be at the Stranraer ferry port. Mrs. Laurie, like us, got lucky.

"I promise you a good night, Mr. Watters," she said on a crackly line.

"Thank you so much," I replied, barely believing we had managed to land a gig on a Monday night. "We've never played Newton Stewart before, Mrs. Laurie. We look forward to playing for you. Good-bye. And thank you."

I put down the phone and slumped back down in the chair.

"God," I said to myself. "My prayer's been answered."

It was time to go and tell the rest of the band the good news.

THE MORNING AFTER

With the ferry terminal only half-an-hour away, and in no real rush, I let the band finish saying their good-byes to their new girlfriends before driving back to Stranraer. Newton Stewart was a great place to play, and our surprising gig there had come as a huge relief to me.

After the gig was over, I slumped down in a chair, relaxed, and savoured the occasion. I couldn't believe how lucky we were to land such a good gig at short notice.

I managed to catch up on some much-needed sleep on the ferry - a measly, but welcome, couple of hours. Now the next hurdle was Belfast. When we got into the city in the early hours of Wednesday morning, I quickly got us on the M1 before noticing that the wagon started stuttering and misfiring as we went up a hill. At the top of the slope, the wagon came to a grinding halt. Damn! It was 5am in the morning, pitch dark, and we were sat on a motorway. But this was no normal highway - this was bandit country. Stuck, there was only one thing to do: flag down the first approaching vehicle. This was a very, very scary thing to do. It was the height of The

Troubles - people just weren't for stopping in the middle of the motorway at some Godforsaken hour to help someone whom could possible be a terrorist. We had no idea if we were flagging down the IRA or the UDA. The Miamis, another showband, would be blown up on this same stretch of road years later. We were all a little more than a bit freaked out by the situation.

Eventually a van did turn up - a bakery van. I explained our situation to the driver and within seconds this fine bloke was helping me to fix the wagon. The problem, he said, was dirt in the fuel lines. Normally a problem that could take some time to fix, within what seemed like a blink of an eye the bakery driver had us up-and-running again, even offering to follow behind us to make sure we were OK. My hands were black with oil from helping him fix the wagon so he gave me a packet of Handy Andies (handkerchiefs) to clean my hands with. What a gent. The bakery driver was indeed a brave man to stop and help us - we could have been terrorists for all he knew – and waved farewell to him when we eventually reached the next town safely.

Later on, though, when we reached Newry on the border, the night silence was broken by the shrill of an ambulance siren, a fire engine on full alert, lights blazing, and an army escort hurtling past us at a horrific speed. Almost immediately I discovered the main road was closed - totally closed. So we had to head for an unapproved road which had been signposted as a diversion. Unapproved roads weren't safe and we could have ended up in serious bother. Within a couple of minutes we soon caught up with a heavy goods lorry before stopping at a junction.

There were no signs or any indication as to where to go next, but my instincts told me to head towards the lights in the night sky, hoping somehow that it would guide us to the next town. Scared witless that we were about to get blown to smithereens, the lorry driver waited for us to drive in front of him before following us, the swine. If anything happened, it was going to happen to us first. He was bigger than us, too! So anyway, we continued along this narrow track road until we eventually came back onto the main Dublin Road. To our horror, there was a car burning in the middle of the highway! First thing I thought to myself was how long had it been there. Was it booby-trapped? So, foot down on the accelerator, I drove up onto the grassy verge, and, head down, went like the clappers and hoped for the best. Much to our relief, we soon got onto a safe road and had no more incidents on the journey home. Phew!

When I arrived back at my mother's house after dropping off the band - our nerves just about intact - my mother came out and met me at the front door looking all concerned and distressed, asking me if I had heard about all the commotion that was happening in Northern Ireland.

"A bomb had been set off at the Army checkpoint," she said, trying not to panic even though I'd made it home safe and sound. "Three young soldiers were blown up. I was so worried about you, Jimmy. I thought something terrible had happened to you."

"Don't be silly, mother," I replied nonchalant as you like. "We never saw or heard a peep."

As we both headed inside the house for a deserved cup of tea, my mother failed to notice the beads of sweat still trickling down my forehead. Luckily I still had one of the bakery driver's handkerchiefs in my back pocket. Handy Andies right enough.

PENTLAND FIRTH HELL

November 1969, and another Scottish tour was almost at an end. Exhausted, in poor health, and about as thirsty for clean water as a Formula 1 car is for petrol (there were no 24-hour petrol service stations in the late '60s), when you're on the road with a showband for a long stretch of time, a month can seem like a year with your mother-in-law for company. Simply put, we were knackered.

Playing every town, city and village hall in Scotland had been utter mayhem. Crushed by autograph-hunting teeny-boppers in Tain, we got pelted by penny-throwing Teds at a gala in Keith. We had a near-death experience involving an out-of-control tractor at an Elgin barn-dance, and played to a bunch of stiffs who barely clapped at all during a performance at the Beachroom Ballroom in Aberdeen.

Now we had arrived in the flatlands of Caithness and the wee town of Thurso - the most northern town on British mainland. A pancake-flat terrain cruelly exposed to harsh, gale-force winds that crushed any few trees there were, the rain came at us horizontally instead of vertically as we literally swept into town. Normally, this pretty coastal settlement could have been any other sleepy town in Ireland, the local accent strikingly similar to folk from Northern Ireland. Yet it was only until we boarded the ferry to Orkney at Scrabster Harbour that it suddenly dawned on us that we were now officially closer to Oslo in Norway, than my hometown of Drogheda in the Republic of Ireland.

We were on our way to a midweek gig in Stromness, before coming back across the water to play Thurso's Viewfirth Club. We had been booked by naval officers who belonged to the U.S. base (it was the height of the Cold War) stationed a few miles west of Thurso. The ferry over was fine. Seeing the majestic sight of the Old Man O' Hoy was impressive, as was the humbling sight of scuttled German warships in Scapa Flow, a kind of graveyard for World War ships, boats sticking eerily out of the water. When we left the boat at Stromness, we were told by the ferry's staff that we had to be back at the port in time for the 7am crossing to Thurso. In other words, we knew not to get too drunk after the gig. But no such luck. After the gig, the band members got very friendly with a few of the Orcadian girls, and sure enough, the dance went on until three in the morning. You could hardly move in the venue for tripping over hundreds of half-bottles of booze –

everyone carried a nip-flaskback in those days. With all the drinking and debauchery going on, we barely had any time to get any sleep before heading off to catch the ferry in the morning.

When we did eventually make it down to the ferry - all bleary-eyed, the skin stripped from our faces by the gale-force winds - we were informed that we wouldn't be able to set sail due to the atrocious weather. I complained profusely to the captain that we had to get to Thurso, as we had a booking there that night. We prided ourselves on honouring all our gigs, and were, if you'll pardon the pun, determined not to miss the next show come hell or high water. The captain, however, simply pointed towards the mouth of the harbour in a sarcastic manner and said, "Look".

Dear God. All we could see were these gigantic, white rollers roaring into the harbour. The captain was adamant that if we sailed in those conditions, the huge waves smashing into the side of the boat would split the boat in two. It was clear to see: we would not be going anywhere. So we all looked to each other as if to say, well, what now? Luckily the secretary (at the club) who booked us in for our Orkney date had insurance just in case a band couldn't reach the mainland due to bad weather after a gig. A lovely woman, she took us back to her house where she said we could stay warm and comfortable until she could arrange a way back to Thurso for us. To her credit, she managed to get in touch with a local fisherman who had gone over to Thurso earlier with his catch. He was due back at Stromness around 4pm, so we were free to hitch a ride with him if we wanted to make our Thursday night gig in Thurso. The catch (no pun intended)? We had to sail in a trawler!

Now this was winter, and there were gale-force winds of biblical proportions to contend with. This part of the world was wide open to the elements where there was virtually no escape from the harsh winds. By the time the trawler arrived it was almost pitch black.

Despite hardly being able to see a thing, we somehow managed to lug all our equipment into the Hold before making our way downstairs to the cabin, huddling round a small table for a cup of watery tea. Meanwhile, our bass player - who was a pale-looking chap at the best of times - was so white he looked like he was about to throw up. And we hadn't even set sail yet!

Within minutes of the boat leaving the dock, his gills were green and he ran up the stairs faster than an Olympic sprinter with ants in his pants. I swiftly followed him to make sure he was OK, but when I got to the deck I got the shock of my life. The Pentland Firth - one of the most underestimated seas in the world, and where the currents of the world's oceans meet - now resembled a scene from the book of Revelations. Waves at least 60 feet high threw us about like a small toy. As the swell made us drop almost 30 feet, I wondered if we would ever come back up. This was the kind of thing I only thought existed in spectacular Hollywood seafaring movies, half-expecting a trident-carrying Neptune to rise up on the backs of giant white horses. It was frightening, absolute horror. I gave up the ghost. We were all goners. We were all going to drown. And for what exactly? A gig in Thurso?

Meanwhile, the trumpet player, in his wisdom, decided to walk along the side rim of the trawler so he could get up to the cabin where the skipper was. What he was attempting to do was about the same as walking a tightrope blind drunk. Yet what he didn't realise was you could have got to the skipper's cabin a more conventional way without having to risk falling overboard. With the waves breaking violently against the boat, and with water spewing out of the port holes at the side, how he wasn't lost at sea was nothing short of a minor miracle.

We were all desperately seasick now. Panic had set in, and I wondered if we would ever see dry shore again. When we all reached the skipper's cabin the crew could clearly see the messed up state of us. To calm us down, they switched on the wireless so we could hear Radio Caroline, and showed us the solar monitoring equipment they used to identify fish in an attempt to calm us down and reassure us. And it did... for about thirty seconds. All of a sudden there was one almighty bang. Boom! Next you knew we were all lying on the floor - including the guy steering the ship. Just like in the movies, the wheel was spinning round like a demented Catherine wheel firework. We picked ourselves up from off the ground and saw that the skipper had begun to panic also, well; we knew we were in big trouble.

"Lights on!" he shouted. "What's damaged?" he demanded of his crew.

Amidst all the confusion and frenetic activity on deck we discovered that we couldn't sail straight because of the way the waves were coming at us, meaning we had to ride the waves piggyback. We got on top of one wave, but there was another one - a freak, second one - right behind it which lifted us right out of the water. That was what caused the bang and our hearts to jump out of our mouths.

With the worst bit over we calmed down a bit, and when we finally touched down on dry land an hour later at Scrabster harbour we all bent down and kissed the tarmac. But there was no time to waste. We had to get into the Hold to fetch our equipment and get to the gig. But what met us there wasn't pretty. All our gear was covered in litres of fishy water, stinking of everything fowl imaginable. Time was pressing on, however, so there was no way we could stop and figure out if it was damaged or not. We had to get going. Before leaving the harbour, however, our singer, Brendan - always the type to have a wee chat with folk, strangers or otherwise - stopped to exchange a couple of words with the skipper before clambering into the wagon.

"Seamus," he said. "I suppose you'll be staying in town to watch the gig tonight before going back to Orkney tomorrow, then, eh?"

"Why, no," replied Seamus, unravelling the boat's ropes from the pier. "We're just going to turn right around now and do a spot of fishing on our way back." Brendan, always ready with a witty reply, was speechless. You could have knocked me down with a feather.

PHFFFT!

When The Viceroys toured Scotland we made a habit of staying at the same digs in every town, city or village we stopped at. Our hosts would often leave a flask of tea and biscuits for us when we got back after a gig. Nice little gestures like that go a long way when you're on the road, especially after a busy show and there's nowhere left open serving food. So when we turned up at our Thurso bed and breakfast looking like something that had just crawled out of the Black Lagoon, our landlady must have thought "My God, what have I got here?"

By rights, we should have had all day to prepare at our B&B in Thurso. But now we had barely half an hour to eat, get washed, get down to the Viewfirth, get set-up, and start playing music.

When we did finally get to the Viewfirth it was like some Confederate mansion with a barn literally attached to the side of it (the "barn" was where the Viewfirth's folk club resided apparently). It sat on top of a hill which gave a glorious panoramic view of Thurso and Orkney. Inside, it was something of a labyrinth: a snooker hall, a dance hall, a badminton court, and a sports and public bar. When we arrived we had to wait until some of the club's members had finished playing their game of bowls in the main hall before we could set up.

Unloading our gear, we all had a heavy feeling in our hearts when we pulled out our equipment. All the canvas covers protecting our amplifiers and speakers were totally soaked through. We all stood looking at each other fearing the worst. Then Sam, our drummer, said what we were all thinking:

"The gear's not going to work, is it, lads? We're fecked!"

As always, the rest of the band turned to me for a solution.

"Look," I said to the rest of the guys, all of them staring at me, arms folded and leaning against the wall. "Let's just plug everything in, switch it on, let it heat up, switch it all off again and see if it dries itself out."

Fine. OK. However, when we came to test the microphones out, as soon as you spoke any sound into them all you could hear was a muffled "phffft" sound. They were knackered. Without any microphones we couldn't play the show. And if there's no microphones then there's no band, and if there's no band then there's no dance, and if there's no dance then everyone will leave, and if everyone leaves then we won't get paid, and if we don't get paid then we can't eat, and if we can't eat then we starve. Good grief! We'd just managed to escape the icy waters of the ferocious Pentland Firth to get here - and now our microphones don't work?

Exasperated, I slumped down on a barstool and buried my head in my hands. Then, out of the corner of my eye, I spotted a Bingo sign. Below it was a battered-looking amplifier and speaker the club must have been using for their Bingo nights. It looked pretty beat up: scratched, covered in tobacco stains, it sounded like a cross between playing through a pillow and a karaoke machine. But, then, what choice did we have?

While we tried to resurrect our equipment from sonic death, people were already beginning to fill up the hall. Five minutes later people were shouting at us to start playing. I could barely understand their thick accents, although in retrospect they sounded quite similar to people who come from the North of Ireland. Whatever they were shouting, they weren't telling us to take our time that was for sure.

Fortunately for us the valves of our amplifiers had dried out - we finally have a show on our hands. The only downside was that when the volume was cranked up the sound started to fizzle a little. Still, we were ready to go. Cue the music, maestro.

Towards the end of the night - during Howlin' Wolf's Little Red Rooster - our singer, Brendan, could barely stand let alone sing, yet people thought his drawl was part of the act and kept sending up bottles of beer to keep us playing. It was the end of a long tour so we thought what the heck and kept on drinking. The music must have sounded a bit slack but the punters didn't seem to notice, or care, they were having a ball.

After the gig - and to save paying money for digs - we made the decision to sleep in the van for a couple of hours before driving straight back down to Glasgow. Mad? Probably. We just wanted to get back to base as soon as possible.

Despite heavy hangovers, and another quick wagon repair, we drove out of Thurso just as the sun was coming up. The locals said Caithness never really got totally dark, and they were right, even if it was November. Heading out of town, we drove down a long road called Princes Street, past the town square, a Georgian bandstand, and the local Picture House Cinema. On the billboards was an advertisement for two films that could not have been more apt to our cause: George Romero's Night Of The Living Dead (which we all looked like) and Steve McQueen's Bullit (which we were about to do down the A9).

The drive back down the road was going not too badly. We got to Inverness fairly quickly. And it was only until we reached the outskirts of Kingussie that Brendan, who was still drunk by the way, asked to be allowed out for a Jimmy Riddle. We stopped at a quiet single-track road, but when Brendan opened the van doors, instead of seeing pink elephants Brendan saw imaginary traffic instead.

"Lads! Lads!" he shouted. "For Christ's sake, I can't go out there! There are loads of cars and Lorries out there - I'll get killed!"

In reality, Brendan was looking onto a Gateway – the van doors opened onto the other side of the main road away from any traffic. Which was just as well, for the sight of a hallucinating Irishman clutching his privates, screaming like a banshee from the side of the road would have had drivers stopping to phone the police had they not crashed their own car first. Brendan – what a character. When we did arrive back in Glasgow we went direct to a service station for our breakfast. By then, Brendan had sobered up, stubbornly refusing to believe he had dodged imaginary cars whilst trying to answer the call of nature.

The tour had sapped the energy out of all of us - we needed a break. When I eventually got back home to

Drogheda, I dumped my bags at the front door and made myself a cup of tea. There's nothing like a good cup of tea after a long tour. Next morning, the phone rang early in the morning - it was Bonici, the Italian promoter from Elgin who often set us up with tours in the Scottish north-east. He wanted us to go another tour.

"Morning, Bonici," I said. "Got another few gigs lined up for us, have you? We just survived the boat ride from hell. Can you give us a wee bit more time to recuperate?"

"Don't worry, Jimmy. Am not calling about a tour in the highlands," he replied. "I need The Viceroys to go on a different kind of tour."

"Oh really?" I retorted, half-expecting him to send us on a Village Hall tour of The Hebrides.

"Jimmy, I want to send The Viceroys to France next year. For six months. Can you go?"

"France?" I squeaked down the phone.

"Oui, oui," came the reply.

DUNDEE DISCOVERY

I'd just returned home from the printers with 2000 copies of the band's new publicity photograph when the phone rang. It was our agent from Glasgow.

"Hello, Jimmy," he said. "I am in a bit of a pickle here. I need you to go to Dundee."

Being called up our agent during the middle of the week usually meant a gig had been cancelled. The director of the agency was also prone to swapping our gigs with other bands at very, very short notice.

"But don't worry, Jimmy – your Glasgow booking's fine. I've got you an extra gig. It's in Dundee, and it's an early show so I need you to get their quickly - by tomorrow in fact."

"Tomorrow?" I remonstrated. "Why? What time do we have to be there? 9pm?"

"No," said our agent. "I need you to be ready to go by 7.30pm."

Now, consider this. Even if we had a private jet available to us there was no way we could get all our gear transported from the Irish Republic to Tayside in such a short space of time.

"That would mean we'd need to leave first thing tomorrow morning," I continued. "It'll take a couple of hours to get to the ferry terminal in Belfast, then another couple of hours to get across the Irish Sea. After that, it's a four-hour drive through Stirling (there was no motorway at the time) before we even get to Dundee."

"Now don't panic, Jimmy," said the agent. "It's extra cash for the band. You'll thank me for it."

An hour later, and after much contemplation, I phoned the agent back and reluctantly agreed to take the gig. The fact of the matter was our agent had us by the short and curlies and he knew it. As amateurs, we had to make a good impression if we wanted to become professional. In other words, take any gig that was offered to us with no complaints, ifs or buts.

By the time we got to Ayrshire the next day, my trombone case and half of our drum kit had already fallen off the wagon's roof-rack in the middle of the countryside. The rack was in such bad nick we had to tie all our gear down with bed sheets. As I picked up our gear from off the side of a single-track road, my face red with frustration, not for the first time I questioned my chosen career path.

We eventually arrived in Dundee at 7pm - 12 hours after we left Drogheda, and with only half-an-hour to spare before show time. Our only instructions: to get to the venue, The Caird Hall, as soon as possible, wherever that was. I'd certainly never heard of it before. We all thought it would be some small, dingy hall on the outskirts of town with just enough room for no more than a couple hundred people. How wrong could one be?

When we got to the Caird Hall we all thought someone had given us the wrong directions. Located in the centre of town, The Caird Hall looked bigger than the Kelvin Hall in Glasgow. It was massive. Like something out of Gotham City, ten Doric Greek pillars, 2150 seats to be exact, and one of the finest Romantic concert organs in the UK. When we got onto its stage we were like dwarves it was so big. You could have fitted a band, a bar, and a dancefloor on the stage it was so gargantuan. The Caird Hall was built for operas and classical concerts, never mind an Irish showband.

A little intimidated by the regal surroundings and with streams of teenagers pouring in through the doors, we were more than a bit unsure we had arrived at the correct venue.

"Is this where The Viceroys are meant to be playing?" I asked a member of staff.

"Yes, they're the main attraction tonight, though there is a small folk group who will be playing during the break. The Viceroys will be on in about 20 minutes."

20 minutes? I looked at the long, dark red, plush rows of seats that came right up to the lip of the stage. Then it dawned on me: we'd never played to a seated audience before. The idea of playing to a crowd looking you square in the eye didn't sound appealing, Caird Hall or not. But this was amazing. You just didn't phone up the Caird Hall and tell them you were coming down to play. We'd never even played Dundee before. The Viceroy of India was probably better known in the city than we were.

Meanwhile, the rest of the band frantically set up the gear as I struggled to take in the environs of this graceful concert hall. A few minutes later I was performing to over 2000 teenagers.

We kicked off the show with a country number, followed by a ballad, a folk song, and a couple of the hit pop songs of the day. We'd got through the first session fine enough, but the reception we received was no better than lukewarm applause. It was weird; eerie. We all looked at each other with concern. I mean, if looks could kill... Everyone was raising their eyebrows and looking to me because I picked the sets. Were we playing the wrong music? I thought teenagers loved rock and roll music. Tanked up on fizzy juice, I figured they'd give us a better reception than simply politely clapping like trained seals. Maybe it was too big a venue to create the right atmosphere? And without a dance-floor, it was like playing to people who'd turned up expecting to see a movie on a cinema screen instead of a showband.

Whatever; during the interval I told the rest of the band to relax, that we were doing the right thing by playing a bit of everything. If the audience didn't like us, well, what more could we do?

Meanwhile, folk duo, The McCalmans, was playing the break in order to give us a break - and from the balcony at that. What was that all about? I'd heard of setting up the stage differently, but to put a band up on the balcony, where they were obscured from the audience's view seemed bizarre to say the least.

No matter, we returned for the second half, played a wide variety of tunes and styles, and again, received light applause. Now these were supposedly wild, rebellious teenagers - teenyboppers who screamed like banshees anytime a rock band came within 1000 yards of them. Now they were acting as if they'd popped round to their grandparents' house for afternoon tea. Talk about being as timid as a mouse.

Then, twenty minutes from the end of the set, a large percentage of the audience got up out of their seats and walked along the corridor at the front of the stage which led them to the exit, stage right. We knew this was a bad gig, but queuing up to leave? Were we really that bad?

A couple of tunes later we noticed a commotion at the side of the stage. There were two bouncers interlocking arms and nodding their heads at me. The entire audience had begun queuing behind them. We simply assumed the throng couldn't wait to get out the hall quick enough. Turned out the bouncers were containing them all.

"What's wrong?" I said to the bouncer, stepping off the stage, trying not to sound too concerned.

"Have you got any autographs you can hand out?" he demanded rather than asked.

At first I thought he was having a laugh, though his facial expression clearly indicated he wasn't.

"Erm, aye, yeah. Why? What's going on here? Do those teenagers want to lynch us? We played all the pop tunes we know."

"These kids don't want to hurt you," he said. "They just want a photograph of the band - signed ones, too. Can you fetch some and hand them out? Please?"

For the next hour or so we sat at the side of the stage applying our signature to three-quarters of the total amount of publicity photographs I had printed up earlier in the week. I had originally expected them to last the entire year. One gig on and it looked as if I'd have to order more. One minute I thought the audience wanted to lynch us, now they were treating us like we were The Beatles or something.

The girls were certainly friendly swapping as many phone numbers as photographs. They demanded records from us, too, even though we didn't have any, and continually asked when we'd be coming back to Dundee to play. Unbelievable.

When we got back to our digs to celebrate, some of us were simply lost for words. This was it. We'd finally cracked it - we were overnight sensations. After all the hard work we'd put in, we were famous, in Dundee at least. They loved us. Yet one thing still baffled me. Why was the audience so polite and reserved? They barely moved a muscle throughout the show; it was like playing to a small town of mannequins. Fortunately, it wasn't until I looked down at the local newspaper - a crass, substitute dinner mat for my late night plate of egg and chips - that it dawned on us why.

One of the news columns reported on something called Mission week. Run by the church, it took in catholic schools, whereby the bishops would give lectures on morality and religion, and the police would give talks on law and order and drugs and all the rest of it. The concert we had just played was their entertainment, their treat. No wonder they were so restrained - they had to set a good example on Mission Week. Well, well, well.

Next morning, I phoned up our agent and told him to book us another show in Dundee as soon as possible. We had to come back and strike while the iron was hot; come back while our name and our faces were still fresh in the audience's mind. No wonder they called Dundee the City of Discovery.

Sadly, an immediate return to Dundee never happened, and we were forgotten about as quickly as we were discovered. Dundee, our agent told us in his wisdom, was just a stopping off point on the way to Aberdeen.

The Caird Hall wasn't set up for bands like us, and anyway, the Mission Week concert was a one-off, a fluke. Dundee supposedly didn't have the big venues and big ballrooms other towns and cities had. So that was that.

Many years later we did return, this time to play a small, grubby dive on the edge of town. We were lucky if we pulled in 200 people let alone 2000. Maybe the Caird Hall show success was a one-off after all. In hindsight, I should have attempted to track down the priest who helped organise the week's entertainment, who am sure, just like the rest of us, loved to have a good old booze up. They'd have booked us back for sure. But that, just like most hard luck stories in the world of rock and roll, is all ifs and buts now.

CRASH!

Three Steps To Heaven. I couldn't get that blasted Eddie Cochran song out of my head.

"I've got some terrible news, Joe. There's been a really bad accident on the drive up to Belfast. I think I'm in shock."

My voice was trembling. I had telephoned Joe, who was in Scotland with the rest of the band, from a phone box just outside Dundalk hospital. My guts felt like they were roasting my other internal organs over a spit.

"Joe, listen. There was a car. It was coming towards me round a sharp bend ten miles out of Dundalk. Teenagers. There were three of them. The road was wet. They skidded coming around a blind corner and ended up flying through the air and into a field. It was a horror scene, Joe. Everyone is in a really, really bad way. Am OK, though. I'll get to the airport and pick you up as soon as I can. I hope am OK to drive."

I climbed back into the wagon, placed my hands back on the steering wheel and started the ignition. What if one of them died? What if they all died?

BOXING DAY BLOOD

Just like St Patrick's Day, Boxing Day is one of the two biggest dates on the Irish calendar, and for us, The Viceroys, our two most important and most lucrative gigs of the year. We were due to play our annual homecoming Boxing Day gig in Drogheda, which was a great honour for us local lads. Playing well and putting on a good show meant getting asked back, and for us, who needed the work and wanted to turn professional, we were up to high-doe getting our chops spruced up for the show. People as far away as Dublin would be coming to see us. Even the locals, who always gave us the most amount of stick, albeit good-natured, were sure to be there ogling us.

The Viceroys had just finished off a couple of gigs in Scotland, the last one being on Christmas Day. Bonici's offer of going to France was a tantalising carrot. I'd casually mentioned it to the band - I was worried some of them might not be able to get the time off from their day jobs - and decided to wait until our next highland jaunt so I could meet Bonici face-to-face to discuss this exciting, if daunting, opportunity for the band.

There was no ferry or plane available to take such a large and heavy amount of equipment back to Ireland on Boxing Day so I offered to take all our gear back to Drogheda in advance (a couple of days before Christmas). To keep the guys playing, I hired a van, some amps and a P.A. for them. So, with the band due back in Belfast around 7.30am on Boxing Day morning, I arranged to pick them up in the van at the airport.

On this particular Boxing Day, however, my dad phoned me up at 4.30am, because, being in showbusiness, I was never able to get myself up in the morning. For once, though, I got up like a shot as I knew I had to get going quick, got in the shower and switched on the radio. As the warm water brought me to life, I couldn't help but sing along to the song playing on the wireless: Eddie Cochran's Three Steps To Heaven.

After the traditional cup of tea and toast, I got in the wagon and warmed her up. It was a cold, still winter morning, a vista of frost blanketing the road like a layer of tiny, sparkling lights. It was ethereal, like a scene from a Christmas Disney movie, not a winter's morning in Ireland. Now on my way to Belfast, I decided to take the quickest route, which meant driving through Dundalk. There was nobody to be seen apart from the local policeman parked at the side of the road as I headed out of town. He was fast asleep on the dashboard so for a bit of devilment I tooted my horn. I didn't stop to see if he awoke.

As I headed for the local hills affectionately known as the Cooley Mountains, I came up a steep hill through some forestry to a bend in the road. Unusual for that time in the morning, a car sped past me flashing its lights frantically.

"What the hell was that?"

No sooner had the thought entered my head, than another car came right round the bend immediately after it. The road was like a bar of soap. The car skidded and catapulted itself right through the air, somersaulting two or three times before crashing into a field just off the motorway and landing on its roof. Time seemed to freeze still. The three passengers inside the car had been shot from the car, discarded like empty crisp packets. The ice was so black I nearly ended up down on the embankment myself.

I got out the wagon and ran over to the crashed car as quick as my size 9 shoes would carry me. The crashed car's wheels were still spinning; the bonnet ripped open as if a huge tin-opener had just prized open a gigantic tin of baked beans. The last thing I expected was to find anyone alive. The car passengers' lifeless limbs were dotted around the field like a humanised version of join-the-dots. I ran to the first person who wasn't making any noise, the lad. He was semiconscious and soon began moaning about his back. He looked barely old enough to drive. I picked him up - you are not meant to pick up accident victims in case you hurt them any further these days, but back then people never thought twice about it - and laid him down in the back of the wagon. He said he could barely feel his legs.

Collecting some blankets, I wrapped them round the other girls. I parked them down and turned up the temperature on the van's heater. They were all badly cut and in deep shock. Their natural blond hair was matted with thick, crimson-coloured blood. One of them, the one who could just about walk, sat in the passenger seat next to me whimpering as she clutched at her chest - she was in total shock. The girl lying across from the lad had tiny incisions all over her arms and legs. She resembled a puffed-up pin cushion and cried like a baby. It sounded like she was calling out for her mother under her muffled moans. There were no such things as mobile phones around at the time, and there wasn't a public phone or house for miles.

Thankfully another car saw us and stopped (they would drive on ahead to Dundalk and phone for an ambulance). Five minutes went by, it seemed more like an hour. Ten more minutes passed and still nobody came. No police car, no ambulance, no nothing. By now I was getting really worried. I could tell they were seriously injured, and I had to get to Belfast to pick up the band. So I switched on the ignition and drove the ten miles back to Dundalk.

Everyone, meanwhile, was still crying and moaning. I didn't have any First Aid on board the van but did manage to stop their bleeding before setting off using some sellotape and some extra towels that were lying in the back of the wagon. At least it was warm inside the wagon, and I gave them some fizzy juice - leftover from our rider from a gig in Dublin a month previously. To try and take their mind of everything, I tried reassuring them we were close to the hospital, and attempted to engage the girl in the front seat in conversation, hoping that some chat might take her mind off the pain she was suffering. I told her I was a singer and trombonist in a band, and began singing Len Barry's One, Two, Three. It seemed to work. She managed to talk a little herself, finding enough energy to comment on how decorative the wagon looked amidst her gentle sobbing. Since I'd bought a new wagon, we decided to turn it into a piece of moving art. The Viceroys' name ran up and down both sides, a shield with a big sword running through it adorning the two back doors. To say we stuck out like a sore thumb was an understatement. At least the ambulance would have no trouble in spotting us.

By the time we reached Dundalk, the sun was just beginning to come up. There was still nobody around; no traffic, no cars, and sure as hell no sign of an ambulance. Fortunately there was an emergency team waiting for us when we arrived at the county hospital. Quick as a flash, staff and nurses whisked the three badly injured teenagers onto trolleys and away into the Accident & Emergency room. No-one at the hospital bothered to ask me who I was, nor was I asked any questions about the crash. I was now irrelevant. Nevertheless, I was pushed for time - I had to be in Belfast super quick.

As I drove furiously out of the hospital car park and onto the bypass, I switched on the radio to try and take my mind of the horror I'd just witnessed.

It was that Eddie Cochran song again.

FEELING GREEN

I arrived at Belfast airport just in time to meet the guys as they were collecting their bags. They were still high from the previous night's gig, nattering about their extracurricular affairs and latest female conquests. I tried, as best I could, to tell them about the car accident but they didn't seem too interested. I guessed they were just focused on getting to Drogheda and playing the gig. Me, though, I was just glad that I had done the right thing and got those poor kids to hospital when I did. As the band loaded up the wagon, I worried about having to face those kids' parents if they died from their injuries. I couldn't get the thought out of my head. I removed a handkerchief from my pocket and wiped my brow, took a quick sip from a bottle of water and switched on the wagon's ignition. It was time to get to the gig.

Backstage at The Boyne Valley Hotel was a hive of activity. Overheated with the crush of bodies, the band dusted down their mohair suits and sculpted their hair. A few burst bulbs dotted around the dressing room mirrors hadn't been replaced since the last time we played here. Even the poster advertising our previous show, stained by tobacco smoke and faded like a T-shirt that had been washed a thousand times, seemed to be holding up the rest of the outdated, mustard-coloured wallpaper together. The band all straightened their ties, buffed their shoes, and took a deep breath. It was almost showtime.

The biggest gig of the year in our hometown, it didn't get much better than that. We'd been keen to go professional and this was our chance to prove it; to prove that we were just as good, if not better, than all the rest of our showband peers. We could skip musical genres like a champion hurdler - country, pop, and soul you name it. If you could hum a few bars of a tune, then we could play it. Sure, we partied hard during the week, but come the time of a show, we were about as sober as a judge on the Sabbath. We had no shortage of girls following us from one town to the next, but we didn't allow girlfriends when we were out on the road. The Rolling Stones we weren't, but we could rock them around the clock when it came time to putting on a live show. The band was rightly exuberant at the prospect of playing in front of their home crowd, but not me. With a film of sweat on my head, I nearly popped a blood vessel when I discovered someone had stolen my green-coloured suit.

"For Christ's sake! I feckin' hate the colour green!" I shouted, knocking over a couple of half-eaten mince pies.

I'd just gone and retrieved my shiny new brown tuxedo for wearing to the gig from the dry cleaners. To match my new threads, the tailor from the store I bought it from (the tux was specially fitted for a compere job I'd acquired at Butlins) insisted on pairing it up with a sleek, green shirt. I reluctantly agreed even though I never liked the colour - a bit of a strange concept coming from a paddy; a bit like saying you come from Scotland but don't like the taste of Irn-Bru.

My dislike for the colour however, was instilled in me by my father, who used to lecture my mother about not buying green clothes, for he believed it brought the Watters family bad luck. In the early '50s, we used to hang our clothes out to dry on a pulley that sat high up and away from the wall in our kitchen. In those days, there were lots of electrical junction boxes all around the house. On one fateful day the electricity had blown the fuse box and caught fire, the wires had melted and dripped down upon my mother's green jacket which was hanging on the pulley. It caught fire, and so did the other coats. In a flash, the whole house went on fire, too. Unfortunately for my little brother Patrick, he got trapped in the house and died from smoke inhalation before anyone could get to him. He was only 7. I was playing in London with The Viceroys at the time when I received the news. Devastated, the colour green would go on to haunt me for the rest of my life, just as much as Patrick's death.

As the band took to the stage and great applause, I waited back in the dressing room for a moment, taking a wee moment to gather my thoughts about the horrific car accident that happened earlier that morning. I was in such a state over our homecoming gig, and so caught up in getting the band organised and ready, I'd somehow managed to shut it out. I sat down on a chair in the dressing room and zoned out as the images of those three teenagers flashed through my head in a series of surreal, blood-soaked visions. Then a rap at the door came.

"Come on, Jimmy," said a member of the hotel's staff, "it's time to rock and roll."

After the two sets were over, a girl in her late teens came up to the lip of the stage with a request she had scribbled in purple lipstick on a ripped up beer mat. She looked really cute and had the most beautiful platinum-blond hair. I swallowed hard as I looked down at her hand-written song request. I felt as if I'd swallowed a match. As we launched into Eddie Cochran's Three Steps To Heaven, I closed my eyes and wished to God those poor kids were all right.

The Viceroys: There's me second from left standing next to Ronnie on guitar. This old photograph was found stuck to a glass frame I had long forgotten about. It's a bit damaged, as you can see.

THE LETTER

A lot of time had passed since the horrific car crash outside Dundalk. Then, one day, out of the blue, a letter arrived with a Belfast postmark on it. It was addressed: The Driver, The Viceroys, Drogheda. It certainly couldn't have been a gig offer, for it would have been easier getting a gig at the Cavern in Liverpool with The Beatles than in Belfast, such was the saturation of showbands in the North at the time. The light, wispy handwriting - clearly a woman's - should have been a dead give-away. The Viceroys didn't receive a sack full of fan mail like teenage pop stars did, but then again it wasn't unusual to receive some appreciative mail in amongst the bills and junk-mail. In fact, this was to be a letter I would remember dearly for the rest of my life.

It read:

"Dear Sir,

We'd just like to write and thank you, the driver, for saving our lives and looking after us at the side of the road last Boxing Day. And for saving us further injury and taking us to the hospital in Dundalk. I, on behalf of the others, will be forever in your debt. We are all well; we have all recovered, thankfully. Joe is fine and walking again after lengthy rehabilitation. My other girlfriend, too, is fully mended also. We're so grateful. Should you ever find yourself in Belfast for whatever reason, you are very welcome to come and see us, where we'll treat you to a night out on the town. We'd be delighted to see you. I, personally, would love to see you.

Kindest Regards,

Rosemary.

Rosemary. It took me all of about a millisecond to realise she was the girl who sat next to me in the van on the day of the crash. How long had it been? Three, four, five, six months? Longer? The events of the crash happened so quickly I'd somehow managed to put it to the back of my mind. Now she'd tracked me down. I could barely believe it. Suddenly the memories of that eventful day came tumbling back in a tidal wave of emotion. I read the letter over and over again before carefully folding the letter and placing it in the drawer by my bedside. My heart lifted for the first time in a long while, and over the next week, I would go return to the letter reading it over and over again. I was so touched by it.

A few months after receiving the letter, The Viceroys were due to start rehearsing again for another Scottish tour. On my way to midweek practice, I stopped the car on the way into town, pulled over by the side of the road and found the nearest phone booth and called Brendan, our singer, to tell him I had to go to Dublin urgently (sometimes I would work in the city as a taxi driver, driving a Hackney cab for extra money if the band had no gigs booked on a weekend). Brendan didn't ask why I was going, but I thought he might have detected a difference of tone in my voice, after all I'd just moments earlier telephoned Rosemary to tell her I was on my way to see her and couldn't stop stuttering. Two hours from now and I'd be at her front door.

Sadly, the times were sad ones. It was the height of The Troubles in Northern Ireland, and driving a southern-registered car around Belfast in the late '60s meant I may as well have painted a huge target sign on the bonnet of my car.

Sure enough, when I eventually tracked down Rosemary's address, it turned out she lived just up the road from the notorious Castlereigh Road Interrogation Centre (very much in the news at the time), run by the RUC, at the top of the Castlereigh roundabout. Such was the paranoia surrounding Republicans in the North, they could have stopped me right there and then and banged me up for six months. I parked the car beside Rosemary's detached bungalow and walked up the path to her door, my heart almost popping out of my mouth. My hands had a film of sweat on them and I felt like I was trying to walk with a glass bottle between my legs. I felt more nervous now than before any other gig I'd ever played with The Viceroys. There was an abundance of expensive-looking cars in the driveway, one of them a golden Jaguar that stuck out from the rest of the cars no better than if it had neon lights attached to it saying "Hey. Look. Over here." Then Rosemary's mother answered the door.

"Hello," she said. "You must be Jim. You're the lad who saved my daughter's life. Please, won't you come in?"

ROSEMARY

When I first clapped eyes on Rosemary I could barely believe it was the same woman I picked up off the side of the road. At the time of the crash she was a bloody mess: clothes ripped; cuts and mascara running down her face; her natural blonde hair entangled by mud and blood. She was quite hefty but now she was as thin as Twiggy on a diet of bread and water. And she was certainly a pure platinum blonde - just like Diana Dors. From her hair to her eyebrows, down to the hair on her arms, she was blonder than a Barbie doll.

She was so genuinely happy to see me when her mother formally introduced us - inside her front door hallway - I was almost overwhelmed with emotion. I didn't know what to say other than give a simple hello. What I did want to know, however, was how she had managed to track me down. She said that she remembered having a chat with me about the band in the wagon. And, that, when she was being put on the stretcher outside the hospital she just managed to catch a glimpse of the wagon as she was being wheeled into the A&E department. Of course! The Viceroys' name was printed on the back of the wagon. That's how she tracked me down.

Just like Rosemary, her mother was also a very kind and warm woman. She had a beehive hairdo that would have made Stella Stevens blush, yet she didn't appear to be one hundred percent sure of me, looking me up-and-down all the time like I was a dodgy insurance salesman who wasn't all he appeared to be. Granted, she was delighted I had helped save her daughter's life, but to come all the way from Drogheda practically unannounced? Well, let's just say I thought it would have been Rosemary's dad (himself, a protestant) who'd be the more suspicious of me - not her mother.

Rosemary's dad was a man's man. A strong, well-built chap with swimmer's shoulders, talkative, he bestowed a weathered face that suggested he'd perhaps seen far away lands in the merchant navy, yet was always smiling, always joking.

At the time, The Troubles were a bloodied blight on our society. I am a Catholic myself, but happy-go-lucky people like Rosemary's dad (himself a Protestant), never seemed to let the Protestant-Catholic issue get in their way. They were above all that kind of stuff.

The late '60s might have brought tension to the North, but it was a great time to be a teenager, especially if you loved music. Elvis, despite his dull-as-dishwater movies, was on the Comeback, looking and sounding better than ever. The Beatles were recording their best work even though they were starting to fray internally. The sounds of the Beach Boys, too, poured from every jukebox in town, while a young, unknown singer called David Jones was changing his last name to Bowie to avoid being confused with Davy Jones of The Monkees.

The Summer of Love showed no signs of entering autumn. It was as if every teenager in the land was hanging out in cafe bars, knocking back milkshakes and firing their pennies into the Wurlitzer jukebox (Acker Bilk's Stranger on the Shore a personal jukebox favourite of mine). Dancehall clubs and their resident groups kept us entertained when we weren't playing ourselves, Wimpy hamburgers were all the rage, beehive hairdos were as common as the cold, and cabaret and miming acts were the in-thing.

At gigs, maple floors were introduced to help move people along during slow dances. Bigger venues had specially sprung floors raised from the ground for jiving and rock and roll dancing. The floor would sit up from the ground, controlled by a mechanism at the side to release or tighten the wood using actual springs. If some rock 'n' roller jumped up-and-down, you had to, as well, or you'd most likely get bounced onto your backside. The whole thing was a novelty for me; there wasn't much like this in Drogheda; it was all cinemas and boring function halls.

So when Rosemary and her pals took me out on the town in Belfast it was a great opportunity to indulge in the teenage culture of the time, as I rarely got the chance when out on the road with the band. After we'd returned from our night out on the town, Rosemary's family insisted I stay at their house. It was strange seeing Protestant and Catholic neighbourhood streets virtually cordoned off from one another, yet travelling back to Drogheda at that time of night, in light of The Troubles, was a very big risk indeed. So I stayed, and slept like a log.

Next morning, Joe, Rosemary's dad, took me out to the back of the house. He was a car salesman, and the back driveway was full of cars, many of which he would sell after-hours.

"You're in showbusiness, Jimmy, right?" he said in a tone that suggested being a musician was a dirty job (it was). "Well, a rock and roll musician like you must have a car. Do you have one?"

I could barely reply before he said "Go on. Pick one - any car you like. It's yours."

Without hesitation I pointed to the golden Jaguar I'd spotted walking up the pathway to the house earlier the day before.

"No problem," he chirped and handed me the keys.

That was to be my first-ever car. Five years later it would be stolen from me in Glasgow.

I saw Rosemary about once every three months after our first proper meeting. The Viceroys didn't get back to Ireland that often now that we were now performing almost exclusively in Scotland (we'd covered more blades of the country's grass than Bonnie Prince Charlie on the run from the Redcoats). Our relationship was purely a plutonic one and we genuinely liked being in each other's company. But as the months passed, the less often we saw of each other.

A couple of years later Rosemary invited me over for her sister, Bernadette's birthday. We hit the local night-clubs before coming back to her house and the party went on for the rest of the night. Everyone was merry and the craic was good. I was a bit worse for wear myself and later on I would be made to feel even worse. As the night drew to a close, I contemplated asking Rosemary out; I wanted to be her boyfriend. Our coming together was a unique happening and because of that we'd become very close. But before I could ask her to be my girlfriend, she introduced me to someone new... her boyfriend. My heart sank. She'd met him a few months previous but never mentioned him to me in case it didn't work out between them. Right there and then both of us knew something had changed forever.

Rosemary's new relationship didn't kill off our friendship, but because of how our friendship had been established and built up, I felt that continuing to visit her would do nothing but impose on her new life with her new man. I had my dignity and I totally respected her.

A couple of year's later I spotted a nib in an Irish newspaper announcing their wedding. Often I would return to the lovely letter she had written me, reading it over and over again. Many a time I came close to scrunching it up and throwing it away, but I simply couldn't do it. That letter of hers really was a life-changing moment for me. So, after Rosemary's sister's birthday party I disappeared from this lovely woman's life just as quickly and dramatically as I had entered it. The years turned into decades and I was positive I would never see her lovely face again.

AU REVOIR AMATEURS

"Come on, then, Jimmy - what's it going to be? Are you in? Or are you out?"

I smiled nervously at Bonici from across his desk. The large Italian promoter with the big protruding smile had always been good to us. I'd never turned down any work he punted our way, and he was always there to sub the band a tenner if we needed it up front. Bonici. An influential man who treated bands who were Number 1 in the Charts no differently than those who formed their first band just last week. He was the first guy to take The Beatles to Scotland, took Pink Floyd to the highlands, and famously told Eric Clapton he'd never play Elgin again following a disastrous gig with Cream. Now I felt as if I was letting him down.

I stood up, walked over to the window of his office, and looked down below at the crackling neon of Bonici's Park Cafe where the band was inside drinking milkshakes.

"I dunno, Albert," I said sheepishly, taking off my glasses. "A girl? I mean, come on, we'd be playing U.S. Air Bases for heavens sake. It'd be pretty rowdy in there to say the least. I've heard lots of horror stories about women getting harassed over there. Those G.Is can be really wild."

Bonici just looked at me, patient, pokerfaced, as if just letting me finish my spiel.

"Plus, we're a compact unit. Bringing someone else in - especially a woman - might open up a whole can of worms. She'd have to get changed in a separate dressing room; she'd have to suffer dirty, smelly men. She'd have to learn a vast repertoire of tunes in a short period of time. You know how it is, Albert. Eh?"

A pregnant pause hovered around the room.

"Well, can I at least go and ask the rest of the band about it first before making a decision? Albert?"

Bonici, looking as relaxed as a piece of overcooked spaghetti, barely moved a muscle in his easy-chair.

"Sure, Jimmy. Go downstairs, grab yourself a coffee and talk it over with the band. Then come back up and tell me you'll take the gig. OK?"

Trudging down the small flight of steps I knew in my heart this was never going to come off. Three months stay in France playing to testosterone-fuelled, boozed up American soldiers - with a female singer fronting the group? I'd been looking for any opportunity to land the band a gig abroad. France is a nice place, but for this type of gig? It all spelt one thing, and it begins with the letter T: trouble.

I'd put off this meeting with Bonici for some time, but why? Was it because I knew he would only offer us the gig if we took on a female singer? Perhaps. For some time now, a few of the other band members had been complaining about taking too much time off from their day jobs to conduct tours with the band. Going to France, I feared, would force some of them to quit our part-time outfit for good. "Au revoir, Jimmy," I could hear them say. It was such a hassle putting The Viceroys together - I didn't want to have to assemble another one from scratch.

Meanwhile, downstairs in the cafe the mood amongst the band was about as exciting as watching a new paint job dry on Ronnie's guitar. Elgin, about 40 miles east of Inverness, might not have been the most vibrant town in the world, but Bonici's cafe always had a certain buzz about it, and not just from the neon sign hanging outside. He practically promoted every showband that came to the highlands, and you were most likely to find them sitting in his cafe, like we were, supping on a Coke bottle and listening to Elvis Presley on the jukebox.

Everyone was a little nervous, no doubt curious as to what I was about to proposition them with - we were in the middle of yet another highland and Grampian tour - so I decided to lighten the mood by recalling our stopover at my aunt's house in the Gracemount area of Edinburgh. We'd travelled up from a gig in Leeds and decided to drop in on some of my family before heading up to the Scottish highlands. In those days I always used to carry two pairs of shoes: one for driving, and one for walking around in. When we got to my aunt's, I was so tired and confused I somehow managed to put one of each shoe on my feet. No-one noticed until my wee cousin, Harry, a sneering spiteful little so-and-so, spotted my mistake when everyone sat down for dinner. "Ha, ha, ha," he'd snort. "James has got two different pairs of shoes on. What an idiot." My face beamed redder than a well-smacked backside. Still, it gave the band a laugh.

As I expected, though, there was no way the members of the band with day jobs could afford to take a month off work to play in France. They would have had to jack their jobs in, and for what? 30 days playing grubby air bases with no guarantee of payment or proper accommodation. ("Non, merci, Jimmy.") Bonici was a man of his word, but in any case the horror stories we'd been reading in the press about showbands performing in Europe scared us. In short, it was just too risky. Ten minutes later I came back down from Bonici's office, told the lads to get in the wagon and headed off to our next gig. As a part-time, amateur outfit, we could not afford the time or the risk of taking on a three-month-long stay in France.

"So, Jimmy, what did you say to Bonici, then?" the rest of the band queried as we drove out into the highland countryside.

"Well, the hard part was telling him we weren't going to go to France. The easy part, however," I said, nonchalant as you like, "was telling him the band will be going full-time. That's right lads - The Viceroys are going pro. Who's in?"

GOING PRO

After the meeting with Bonici (and on the way back to Ireland) I decided that, sink or swim, we were going to turn professional. Our triumphant gig at the Boyne Valley Hotel had proved to me we could cut it at the top level. It was time to stand on our own feet. Cut the apron strings. Do it our own way. Turning down offers to far-flung, more exotic gig locations (bad idea or not) was not a nice feeling. Plus, having invested all my own money in the wagon, advertising and attributing a new PA, one gig a week just wasn't enough to sustain a living.

The harsh reality was we didn't have the same clout as the big boys who were putting out records, living off financial handouts from their respective labels. Some of the band members had wives and children, as well as regular jobs, so I had to entice younger musicians, who, like me, wanted to gig (work) as much as possible. Picking them up and dropping them off after gigs (the band members lived within a 25-mile radius of Drogheda) had become a tiresome, tedious task, so having them on the road all the time was far more suitable and convenient. Just like The Monkees, we needed our own place to live in, too. So, where else should be bunk up? Why, Newton Stewart, in the south-west of Scotland, of course.

As fate would have it, on the journey home from the Scottish highlands we had to drive through Dumfries where, some ten miles or so out of town lay the Auchinlarie Holiday Park. The Park rented out mobile homes, so, on a whim, I stopped the wagon just outside it, got out, and knocked on the owner's door to enquire just how much a mobile home would cost. The park, much to our initial disappointment, was only licensed for the summer months, but Frank - the owner - took pity on us and said we could have an 8-berth down at the bottom of the site, located under trees, on the edge of a cliff overlooking the harbour. There, we would be out of sight.

The nearest town, however, was four miles away in Creetown, which had a population of about 700 and was where Sir Walter Scott laid part of the scene of his novel, Guy Mannering. Another four miles from that lay the small seaside town of Gatehouse. We were stuck in the country, far from essential supplies (tea bags and sausage rolls) and civilisation (a pub with a public telephone). Fortunately, the caravan site had a shop where you could buy milk, rolls, poultry, newspapers and other such sundries. What swung it for us was that it was: (a) affordable; (b) we had a decent roof over our heads; (c) it was secure; (d) we were reasonably close to Stranraer for getting to Ireland.

For the past month or so, myself and the sax player (who also owned a car) had taken to leaving our cars in Belfast, picking up our wagon - which we left with all our gear inside - at a hotel in Stranraer. It was a sensible decision: it saved money taking the wagon over on the ferry, and any time we had to play a show back in Ireland, we knew we could leave the wagon safe under lock and key.

Out in the sticks, and freezing cold in the middle of a bitter, harsh Scottish winter's night, we unanimously agreed that this little caravan park should be our Scottish base. The following Tuesday, I bid a fond farewell to my parents before collecting the keys to my new home from Frank. With the pubs closed at 10pm and four miles away, there wasn't much to do on our first day as official Scottish residents other than unpack our stuff into the berth. Frank, however, had other ideas.

"Guys, I reckon you should throw a housewarming party," he suggested.

"Who would we invite?" I said sarcastically. "Cows from the nearby field? There's no-one around here for miles."

Frank, who always had an answer for everything, wasn't to be outdone.

"Well, first thing we should do is go down and see Eddie. Eddie works on a farm just down the road and is into music in a big way. You've got a portable record player, guys, right? Well, Eddie has every soul record imaginable. Otis Redding, Wilson Pickett, The Isley Brothers - you name it. We can borrow some of his records so we'll have music to listen to."

"That's all fine and well," I retorted "but what about girls? You can't have a party without any girls now, can you? Unless Ronnie plans on putting on a skirt, I doubt we'll see many of them around here."

"Ye of little faith," said Frank, stepping out of the caravan before heading back up the hill to his house.

Within a few short minutes Frank came back. He had been on the phone and tapped up all the girls he knew between the ages of 17 and 21 who lived in the local area. Surprised, but understandably buoyed by this exciting news, we headed into the village to buy enough booze and food to supply a small army. Back at the park, we never made so many sandwiches in our life (ham, cheese, egg and mayonnaise - you name it, we made it) and by 7pm everything was ready for a right old knees up. But where were our guests?

An hour later, and with a bellyful of sandwiches and a suspiciously sulphurous smell wafting in the air, there was still no sign that anyone would show up.

"Maybe Frank was having us on?" said Ronnie, dejectedly, swilling on a bottle of beer.

"Yeah, probably," I replied, reaching into one of Eddie's record boxes trying to find a decent tune to spin on the turntable.

Munching on a tuna sandwich in a caravan in the middle of nowhere, listening to Otis Redding's Sitting On The Dock Of The Bay seemed a world away from where we were currently sat.

Ten minutes later, the flash of headlights lit up the park, a fleet of cars - all 10 of them - came roaring down the hill. The car doors burst open and out spilled the girls Frank promised would come, all of them laughing and chirping away to one another as they entered the caravan. We were all strangers to one another, and as the Lindas, Samanthas and Jackies came in and sat down, a strange, awkward silence filled the air. Yet when one of the girls did open her mouth to speak it was almost impossible to understand the fast, twang in which they spoke.

"My eens! My eens are sair," one of them moaned, which, according to Frank, our Scottish translator, meant her eyes were sore.

Language differences aside, once we all got tucked into the grub, necked a few drams and got the music blaring, a wee bit of a jig ensued on the wee sliver of kitchen lino that doubled as our makeshift dance-floor. To the girls, we were minor pop stars, hence their, initial silent reaction (which is, ahem, understandable when in the company of professional musicians). But once the cogs were well oiled with alcohol they genuinely seemed thrilled to be hanging out with a bunch of paddies with guitars. We certainly weren't complaining.

By midnight, the crowd had started to shrink. With more caravans nearby (empty and open), one by one, people paired off, whereas the less romantically inclined, flaked out on the caravan floor, sozzled. An hour later, drifting off to sleep on my first official night living away from home, all I could hear was a light breeze outside, the waves crashing onto the rocks a couple of hundred feet below the cliff - and Austin our trumpet player's snoring! Five hours later, Austin woke up in a disorientated stupor, although still in party mood.

"Am not having this," Austin muttered to himself, removing his trumpet from its case before deciding, in his alcohol-fuelled wisdom, to give us a drunken rendition of The Last Post.

Not exactly his best-ever performance, it's not certain whether Austin went back to sleep without his trumpet inserted where the sun don't shine. However, it wasn't long before the heads began to appear from the nearby caravans once the birds started tweeting. The girls woke up with smeared make-up all over their faces, steadied themselves, kissed their new-found friends and left as quickly as they arrived.

The rest of us, however, went back to our original bunks, and didn't wake up again until 3pm in the afternoon. Later on, as our popularity in the town grew we found ourselves responsible for our female patrons at the end of the night after a gig. Female fans of the band would be standing outside wherever we were playing sometimes at 1am with no transport to take them home. We lived in a rural area after all, so getting stuck in the middle of nowhere could be a cold, unsettling experience. Being the kind gent I am, I gladly shuttled as many as I could fit in the wagon home. Once I had 30 women squeezed into the wagon, practically sitting on top of each other, but I think they used to enjoy the experience – they all knew they would all get home safe.

Word of mouth soon spread that this local Irish band was a good quality act, personable, and now responsible for taking people home after the show. Our first Easter in town also meant the beginning of the caravan season. With caravans swiftly booking up, Frank was under pressure to move us on. So he put us into two, smaller vans. Cramped, stinking to high heaven, and possibly violating any number of health and safety laws, what made it bearable was the craic we got with all the various holidaymakers and travellers who passed through the camp.

Once the season was over, though, we got to move back into our original caravan. By now our faces were regular fixtures in the area, and it wasn't long before we came into contact with a lovely woman who cleaned the caravans in the camp. She owned a couple of houses in nearby Creetown, whereby she offered us a two-storey house on the condition we rented it out all year round. At £20 a week we had found our new home for the next two years.

Yes, life in Creetown was certainly quaint and idyllic. We got to know the local police, the hotel owners and even those who worked at the one-and-only garage in town on first-name terms. Like most small towns though, everyone knew our business: if someone found out you had a cold, two hours later it would have manifested into intestinal flu. Still, the people there were great towards us and always greeted us with a warm smile and a hello. Marina, a delightful Italian man who ran the local cafe, always made sure we got a hot roll for breakfast on weekend mornings.

Even the local football club did us a star turn when we enquired about using their social club's hall for rehearsing in. We initially suggested that we play a midweek gig for them, which, unfortunately, they initially refused at first because they couldn't afford to pay us. So I said if they ran the hall and put stewards on, we'd take a percentage of the door take instead of them having to present us with a fee.

Tommy Truesdale, a DJ on Radio Ayr and who also had a Scottish band on the go, always drew a crowd in the town. But apart from Accordion Trios there was little else in the way of live entertainment. So we were in. The committee agreed to stage the gig; their wives turned up to make tea, soup and sandwiches, and just about the entire town turned up for what was a great night of music and dancing. My only problem was getting the band away from the bar and keeping them onstage. By the end of the night, though, the club secretary said the gig had been a roaring success, taking only £50 for the football club and giving us £100, which, in fairness, was far more than we deserved.

However, I must say, during this gig - and like many other shows we performed in the town - I'll always remember the audience begging us to let one particularly notorious chap join us onstage to sing a song. This guy was always drunk, and he was no different this night. But it was a good laugh, and this little party piece really endeared us to the locals. They looked at it as if they were part of what we did, and in a way they were. To this day I can still hear some of them singing with us as they did many, many years ago. We might have been living a long way from our hometowns, but Creetown treated us all like locals.

We were gigging every weekend, midweek gigs were not too difficult to come by, and we were even finding gigs on Monday evenings, too. Some of the local halls were easy to hire so if a Friday booking didn't materialise, with the help of the football club - who would steward and run the event for us - we'd be in good hands. Then there was the Lybro Jean Factory in Dalbeattie with about 4000 workers: if we needed a crowd to help fund a local dance, one phone call to the factory was all it took to help spread the word.

My decision to turn us into a full-time, professional band was paying off. Having settled The Viceroys' ship, it was now time for us to progress to the next level... getting us on TV.

HELLO GLASGOW

The first time we played Glasgow as a professional band was an unsettling experience. Arriving on a dark night, the city was surrounded by thick fog; big, black, grimy tenements that seemed to tower in on us like some mammoth from a '50s monster movie. It was quite daunting for us lot who had grown up in small, idyllic Irish towns. Glasgow was a sharp shock to the system all right. Pubs closed at 10pm, dancing stopped at 11pm on a Saturday night (we were used to people dancing until 2am in the morning), and the only way you could get a drink on a Sunday was if you went to a hotel. Even most of the shops were closed. Saying that, Glasgow's people were very friendly and welcoming towards us.

Our first gig there took place on a Tuesday night at a huge cinema theatre that had been converted for bingo when there wasn't any live music on. Early week gigs were like gold-dust, and though we never dreamed we'd end up playing a bingo hall, despite playing to a slightly older crowd than our usual age group, they were very sweet, and often assured us they would take their families and friends along to see us next time.

By the time we got back to our digs and into bed it was fast approaching 4am. It seemed like my head had barely hit the pillow when I was woken up again by loud shouting in the street outside, the perpetrator screeching in a rough, foghorn-loud, voice. I couldn't make out what was being said as it simply didn't make any sense. Who was it? Was there a fight going on? No, it was the coalman! The tenements we were staying in were four-to-five stories high, so instead of climbing the stairs to rap on peoples' doors, the coalman would simply shout out to the women who were sitting on the windowsills ready to shout down their orders. I'd never heard or seen anything like it in my life before. Welcome to Glasgow, Jimmy.

However, if we thought playing to a bingo audience was bizarre, then the next night's gig at the Singer Sewing Club really took the needle and thread. Located in Clydebank, and with a workforce of over 10,000 this strong-willed community had their own complex that doubled as a social club. It was very popular, and you were always assured of a big, good tempered audience. It was like a town within a town. Then we discovered that our weekend gig in the Gorbals was in actual fact a former Jewish synagogue converted into an Irish club by Irish entrepreneurs. An unusual place to play, every hobo under the sun turned up here. From IRA men to local thieves and the mafia - you name it they were here. Usually we'd start around 10pm and get off stage around 2am. The plus side though, was we could keep all our equipment on stage as we were usually booked there for two nights, even if it meant having to protect our belongings with barbed-wire and booby traps to ward off any potential thieves.

The hippy movement was still in full flow (or should that be full blow?) with almost every student we played to at the Strathclyde University and the Albert Ballroom stoned out of their heads on dope, sitting cross-legged to watch the gig. Every time we played to them all you'd get was "Cool, man. Groovy. Yeah, baby. Outta sight." We weren't into that whole scene at all, yet under the Albert Ballroom was a disco named Joannas where The Viceroys could often be found blowing off their own kind of steam after a gig.

Glasgow, though, as anyone who lives in Outer Mongolia or on the dark side of the Moon will tell you, is famous for its two major football clubs, Celtic and Rangers. In Glasgow there were no grey areas: you either supported one or the other. Being paddies everyone assumed we were all Celtic supporters, which was true; but we weren't that much into football, and it certainly didn't stop us performing gigs at Celtic and Rangers' Supporters Clubs, often playing RSC in Govan on a Sunday afternoon before heading to Parkhead and playing the CSC later at night. We were humble musicians; we didn't care about anyone's religion, nor did we expect our audiences to care what ours were, either. You don't upset the apple cart.

A chap named Ross Bowie, meanwhile, who was a big Glasgow promoter and who put on the likes of The Alexander Brothers, often put us on in the Rangers' Supporters Club in Govan. A grand building full of plush, soft furnishings, it was a stark contrast to the right-down-to-earth, take-it-or-leave-it surroundings of the Celtic Supporters' Club. Whenever we negotiated a fee with those who ran the CSC club, their biscuit-tin mentality always ended in conversations about how they could find a band to play for £20 instead of paying us the going rate of £40. Nevertheless, the gigs there were raucous, high-energy affairs with women dancing on the tables, and pints sent up to us to keep us playing.

During the early '70s, we often played the Clelland Miners Welfare in Lanarkshire, where we were often warned by the club's committee members not to strike up any rebel songs, only for the committee themselves to come up and ask us to play them after they'd polished off a dozen pints or so. Sam, our drummer, had a party piece where he would (with faux naivety) ask the patrons of the club what type of music they liked. They'd tell him to get us to play God Save the Queen, which for us - Catholics from the Republic of Ireland - would have been like asking King Billy if he had any Rosary beads on him. That said, we never had any bother in either Rangers or Celtic Supporters' clubs - ever.

The place for bother was at the American Base in Dunoon, a floating base (not on British soil) just off the south-west coast of Scotland. The white and black southerners hated each other with intense passion. The MPs - Bubbleheads as we called them - struggled to keep order every time we came to play for them during the late '60s and early '70s. The blacks shouted for soul music, jitterbugging on the dancefloor, their eyes flashing wildly. The whites, on the other hand, would be screaming at us to play Johnny Cash, whooping and hollering and hurling beer every time we played a country and western number. It was tit for tat. Luckily for us, we could play both styles of music to keep both camps contented, albeit momentarily. They fought like cat and dog, and I thought Rangers and Celtic fans didn't like each other.

A little further out of Glasgow however, lay something a little more serene: The Duck Bay Marina, in Balloch, Loch Lomond, which goes down as one of the nicest places we ever played, a lovely venue am glad to say is still there today. Teenagers and people around our own age group (mid-twenties) would come to see us perform there, and from the stage you could look out the big, glass windows and see all the moored boats all lit up, bobbing up and down in the water. The only drawback was that the stage was the size of a dog kennel. Worse, it was up behind the bar and above the gantry, so every time someone in the band took off on a ripping solo there was a chance they might fall six feet onto one of the bar staff below and spend a month in a body cast.

When we were still semi-professional we conducted a tour of England, mainly in the North East and London area playing 30 nights in a row. Three days before we were due to commence the tour one of the band's guitarists couldn't get the time off to play. Enter Matry Ford. Highly regaled by local musicians in Drogheda as well as further a field, the rhythm guitarist and singer was a one-man show in his own right. Luckily he was available and willing to join us.

The main club we played in London was called The Gresham. This was the only venue that would give Monday night gigs to visiting bands. You were lucky to get booked there once a year. Traditionally, Monday night was the night off for nursing staff, so it was billed as a nurses' dance, and therefore always attracted a crowd as nurses guaranteed loads of men turning up. It was a great venue to play. It had a revolving stage, and there was atmosphere about the place that made you feel...special. While the resident band played the warm-up slot, we would be just behind the backdrop on the other stage setting up. So when the time came for us to begin we would be introduced by the announcer before slowly revolving round to greet a crowded room. It was a bit like how contestants on Blankety Blank were introduced, and the audience reacted to us brilliantly. However, they fell dead silent whenever we played any songs Marty sang on. Not because he was awful. On the contrary, whenever Marty flexed his vocal chords everyone in the room stopped dancing and listened intently as a way of showing their appreciation.

Marty was big on the ballads especially Roy Orbison ballads. Boy could he hit those high notes. During The

Gresham show there was an emotional Irish ballad we played that seemed to cast a spell on everyone in the room who heard it. The song was based on a story about an Irish priest from Wexford who led an Irish uprising against the English using only pitchforks, hammers and picks to fight them with, scoring a famous victory against the opposing armed forces. Afterward, someone came up to congratulate us - Marty in particular - on our performance, and asked us if we would oblige them by providing them with the lyrics. It was our pleasure.

Our wagon, incidentally, only had three seats in the front and Marty loved to sit on the middle one, chirping away to all who would listen to him. On journeys after gigs, Marty would often sing as well. It was great for keeping we awake at the wheel. What I didn't know was he had itchy feet. One morning I awoke to find his bed hadn't been slept in. His bag was missing, his guitar was also gone. He had taken off without any warning, no excuses, not even a note of explanation – nothing. It was the last I saw of him for years. His friends later told me he was renowned for doing this kind of thing, having run out on bands during tours numerous times before. He just couldn't stay away for any length of time. Roots and responsibility supposedly scared him. In short, he was afraid of commitment.

Years later he walked into the music agency office I was working in on Bath Street in Glasgow. He was looking for work. It was a pleasant surprise to see him, and soon enough I was helping arrange gigs for him. A recording deal with the budget LP label, K-Tel Records was in the offering. We had to get him to sign a contract to protect his and our interests. But no, he would not commit. He was happy just gigging a couple of nights a week so he could return home every night. There was not one doubt in my mind that had he been able to commit, Marty Ford would have taken the place of Sidney Devine and Daniel O' Donnell. It was a shameful waste of talent.

A few months prior to moving to Scotland, we played a gig in the far flung regions of rural West Ireland - Doohoma to be exact. It was such a small place it wasn't even on our road map, and getting there from Drogheda meant a 250-miles-there, 250-miles-back round trip. At that time the UK and Republic of Ireland was still very regional. People hadn't really started to travel, not as we know it now. There were no big motorways, let alone decent roads in rural Ireland. But when you're stuck for a Sunday night gig you'll go almost anywhere.

So there we were: driving along single-track roads, 60 miles from the nearest town, and hoping that there weren't any werewolves hiding behind any bushes waiting to pounce on us. Then, just as we were debating the Doohoma's very existence, out of the darkness, down a big slope just off the road we could just about see the letters D-O-O-H-O-M-A slapped on the side of the hall we were due to play. We had arrived.

Despite the dark and wet weather, a lovely, very homely woman greeted us at the door with tea and biscuits, even though she was just as surprised as us to have found the right location. As we unloaded our gear onto the wooden-floored stage you could tell the hall only opened its creaky doors once a week due to the smell of old, tatty seats and burning dust from the vintage-looking radiators. By the time we got on stage at 10pm there was a small amount of people inside the hall, most of them having arrived on specially buses that came from 20 miles in each direction.

I kicked off our set singing some Manfred Mann and Cliff Richard songs, Joe taking over lead vocal duties to sing some country tunes by Kenny Rogers and Willie Nelson.

Sam, our drummer, was excellent at vocal harmonies, and would often do some Beach Boys numbers and Four Seasons stuff, maximising his rippling falsetto to fine effect. When it came to folk music, Austin, our trumpet player, would lay down all The Dubliners and Clancy Brothers tunes.

As the old cliché goes, we literally had something for everyone. By quarter to midnight, however, there was still hardly anybody there at all. Our hopes were raised momentarily when the attendance surprisingly increased. But instead of frisky women it was a flock of sheep who had taken a wrong turning instead. "Good God," I said to myself as we trotted through another country and western number. We'd had more hot dinners than there were people standing in the audience, which was saying something. No way were we going to make a shilling from this gig. Imagine our surprise then, when, almost exactly on the stroke of midnight, a huge squad of people - probably everyone who'd been chucked out of the nearby pubs at closing time - came thundering into the hall like a host from Hades carrying pitchforks. It was mad. On one side of the hall were all women, men lining the other side. Dressed in big, frilly dresses, their hair all bunched up nice and neat, the farmers' daughters in the room were all big, strapping girls. Pretty they were, too. With the band in full swing now, Joe shouted at me from across the stage:

"Where the hell did those women come from?" he said, trying not to stray out of time with the music.

"Jimmy - they're beautiful."

He was right. They were all attractive. Though I couldn't understand how they looked so healthy. Doohoma was a remote place, but the grass wasn't exactly lush. There was barely enough grass for a donkey to eat, let alone breed any cows or sheep. Still, we weren't complaining.

At 2am it was time to pack up, say our good-byes again and head for home - whichever direction that was in. Three hours later bumping over single-track roads, my eyeballs were almost hanging out of my head. By the time we arrived in Drogheda, everyone was on their way to work as were getting to our beds. Stumbling back into my parents' house with all the grace of a drunken giraffe, I had just enough time to say hello to my mum and dad - who were chewing down on their cornflakes - before heading to the land of nod.

"Jimmy," my father said, as I trudged wearily up the stairs to my old bedroom.

"You've got a letter here. It looks important."

"If it's Apple Records asking if am going to join The Beatles, tell them am not interested, will you?" I said, sarcastically, kicking the bedroom door open with my trombone case.

I slumped down face first onto the bed. Two seconds later, a rap at the door. Dad:

"It's got the Borders TV emblem on it. The postmark says Carlisle. I think you should open it now, Jimmy," my father insisted.

I tried to open my eyes, half-heartedly trying to compute what my father was saying. Borders TV? Carlisle? Then the penny dropped. Of course - I shot up out of my bed - Opportunity Knocks.

Doohoma: The village hall as it is today.

OPPORTUNITY GONE

It was twelve months after we had first applied to appear on Opportunity Knocks that a letter confirming our audition finally arrived through the letterbox. One of the most famous and longest-running television talent shows ever, Opportunity Knocks was one of the most popular TV shows around, and a forerunner to today's Pop Idol and X-Factor (so-called) talent shows.

It had been such a busy time for The Viceroys, the entire band - myself included - had all but forgotten about our application. For a second I thought the letter was a wind-up sent to us by another showband, for in those days getting on TV was about as easy as getting a return flight to the Moon. No TV studio or radio station in the land would consider giving you any air time, or put you on their roster if you were trying to attract a booking agency without performing an audition first. You just couldn't turn up with your guitar and expect to be given a tryout. No chance. That wasn't acceptable. The people in control of the music industry were serious men: you had to have more than just a degree of talent to even dream of being considered.

Despite our forgetfulness over the application, however, we did try to watch Opportunity Knocks every chance we could. After all, it had the power to make or break careers.

So the day came: Wednesday. A midweek date, it was ideal because we weren't playing anywhere that particular day. We got out of our beds early and headed for the Borders Television studio in Carlisle where we had to be at 2pm. There were a couple of other groups already there when we began lugging our gear in, one of them a local heavy rock group.

The studio was like a small aeroplane hangar: cold, grey, gargantuan, bare without the technicians and TV cameras to fill up the space. All the acts scheduled to audition were all set up in a circle - like you see on Later with Jools Holland - each act positioned within a few feet of one another. To our amazement, Hughie Green - the wisecracking presenter and star of the programme - played an active part in the auditioning process and was quick to have a craic with us just because we were Irish.

"You going to play us some Leprechaun music today then, eh?" he'd gobble in a terrible Irish accent, ignorantly unaware of how stereotypical he sounded. "Come all the way from Ireland have you? You must be a folk group, I suppose?"

We all tried not to cringe.

"Oh no, not at all," I retorted, speaking on behalf of the band. "We play pop music, as a matter of a fact."

No sooner had the words left my lips Hughie was already making another wisecrack, this time at the expense of poor Ronnie (more about him later) and his height, or lack thereof.

Despite his cruel putdowns, to be fair, Hughie could be tremendously charismatic, and the fact he was willing to come down and mix in with everyone prior to the audition put us at ease and earned everyone's' respect. So we sat around the studio and watched the first act - the heavy metal band - audition.

They weren't what you might call fantastic, or the sort of band that would make for compelling TV viewing, nevertheless they were all right at what they did: making a huge racket in a Black Sabbath kind of way. Though we weren't initially competing with the other bands and acts the audition was essentially a straightforward process just to prove you could actually play. Sounds easy, doesn't it?

Now Joe our bass player, who was the eldest, always used to get on at Ronnie, who played lead guitar in the band. A week before we headed down to Carlisle, Joe kept on at Ronnie so not to forget to bring spare guitar strings.

"Now, Ronnie, you're going to remember to bring spare guitar strings to the audition with you, aren't you?" Joe would repeat. "We can't be going all that way without you having spare strings. We wouldn't want any of them to snap now, would we?"

"Yes, yes," Ronnie would snap back at him.

"Stop worrying, Joe, will you, I've never let us down in the past - have I?"

Well, that was the kiss of death, wasn't it? When we got to Carlisle, sure enough, Ronnie broke a string as we were all tuning up. He dipped his hand into his guitar case where, low and behold, there were no spare strings. Pushed for time, he attempted to tune the remaining five strings on his guitar when ping! He snapped another one.

Joe, as you might imagine, waded into Ronnie.

"For Christ's sake, Ronnie, I knew this would happen!" he boomed. "How many times have I told you to bring spare strings?!"

Ronnie was livid.

"I know, I know, Joe," Ronnie stammered trying to keep his cool. "I normally buy strings during the week before our weekend shows. I never had time to go this week as we had to come down today, the same day I usually buy my guitar strings."

Suddenly things got a whole lot worse. During our soundcheck, the bass, rhythm and lead guitars all sounded fine (Ronnie had to make do by playing the four bass strings on his guitar), however when the brass section was brought in everything sounded out of tune. Nightmare.

In hindsight, the decision to tune the brass (trumpet, sax and trombone) to the guitars was the wrong idea - it should have been tuned vice-versa, or, to a piano. We tried tuning up again but, under pressure to get ready for our performance, the stress messed with our concentration resulting in everything now sounding almost a semitone out of tune. Then Hughie Green came over to us and told us to start playing. A bead of sweat trickled down my forehead, as the rest of the band shuffled nervously into position. Ronnie looked like someone being led to the electric chair. We started off with a pop number and all was going not too badly. Being slightly out-of-tune gave the overall sound a chorus effect, which though not exactly harmonious, wasn't exactly too uncomfortable to listen to, either. Then we cracked into a country and western number.

Oh dear. As soon as the brass came in with the guitars I screamed "Oh My God" to myself in painful silence - it all sounded flat. We played on but even the most tone-deaf person in the word could have heard how woefully out-of-tune everything sounded. We all looked at each other with deep-rooted fear in our hearts. Just fifteen minutes earlier we were joking about how decidedly average the band who went on before us were. Who were we to talk now? This was tripe, total and utter tripe. And everyone in the room knew it. We could see the other band smiling to themselves. The judges, Hughie Green included, merely raised their eyebrows as if to say "What a disaster." We didn't even get the chance to finish the last song before Green shouted "Next, please!"

Dejected, we trudged meekly offstage, our heads bowed, packed our instruments into their cases as quickly as possible and headed for the studio Exit doors. It was barely 4pm when we left Carlisle for home. I felt physically sick.

On the way back to Scotland not one single word was spoken inside the wagon. This was highly unusual for a lot like us, always joking or chattering on about something or other. In fact, there was no sound other than the hum of the wagon's engine and the drumming of knuckles on the side doors. If anyone said anything then it certainly didn't register with me. Joe wasn't speaking to Ronnie. Ronnie wasn't speaking to Joe. Ronnie was embarrassed. I was embarrassed. We all were. Our sax player, Billy, however, was the type who would try anything - no matter what wrong had been done, or how tense a situation was - to restore harmony (no pun intended) by offering some diplomacy. He made a half-hearted attempt to open his mouth but was stopped in his tracks by Joe who raised his hand as if to say "Don't even bother, pal."

The disaster at Borders' Studios was really hard to take. To apply an ugly pun on it all, we had just knocked the opportunity to appear on Opportunity Knocks. If we knew we were completely useless then the rejection would have been a lot easier. I mean, had Hughie Green said "Look, lads, you can't knock two tin cans together" we'd have accepted it. Had we even just got past the first round, a second appearance on TV - no matter if we'd been bombed out - would have gathered us a tremendous amount of publicity. We already had a decent reputation in Ireland and Scotland, and we were good at what we did. Unlike nowadays it was so much harder to get on the television back then. The tiniest amount of exposure could have opened up so many doors for us. People would have been talking about us, bookings would have doubled, and other work would have steamrolled in. There was nothing surer. The door of opportunity, however, had been cruelly slammed in our face, the carpet pulled from underneath our feet.

Back home, it was days before anyone could speak to each other. There was a big black cloud of depression hanging over all of us. We knew we had blown a big chance. In fact, it almost destroyed us as a band. Morale was lower than a pregnant ant. When were we going to get another opportunity like that again? Would another opportunity like that ever come around again? The immediate feeling was "Should we even stay on the road?" The trauma of it all plagued me like a bad cold that refused to run its course. On Opportunity Knocks' auditions, all you had to do was show you were competent; stay in tune; show them you could operate as a tangible band unit. Had we done any of those simple things, we'd have sailed through the audition. It wasn't as if we were competing with the other acts. Sure, there would invariably be other male and female singers and comedians in amongst the line-up competing with each other, but being in a band always put you ahead of them right away.

In the end, we never told any of our friends or relatives that we had auditioned for Opportunity Knocks let alone told them we'd applied. For a start, we never even thought we would be invited to audition. Secondly, who would have had the balls to explain our failure to everyone if we never got through to the television appearance stage? It was one secret I'm glad we kept. With egg on our faces, we'd have been laughed out of the little village we stayed in.

However, when it came to playing our next gig (in Preston) we automatically switched back into the old mode again: How long would our set have to be? What kind of an audience would we be playing to? What time did we have to load-in by? After the first set was over, everything was back to normal. It was as if we'd realised our one and only opportunity had come and gone, and that the only way to deal with it was to pretend it never happened at all. However, at the end of a long, yet reasonably enjoyable set, as we walked off stage I could tell I wasn't the only one thinking our crack at the big time had failed all because of a guitar string and some badly-tuned instruments.

Funnily enough, Ronnie never did forget to buy spare strings in future.

SNOW JOKE

After the Opportunity Knocks disaster it was a slight consolation that we were booked to play The Hibernia in Preston, one of our regular bookings in England. Although it was in the north of England, it was within two hours travelling distance from our Scottish base, and not far from the M6 motorway. Sunday night bookings, as am sure you're now fully aware, dear reader, were as rare as hens' teeth north of the Border. If you did find one it was usually poorly paid, and the club was usually small and cramped. As luck would have it our first gig at The Hibernia came to us by pure chance. Another band pulled out at the last minute which resulted in a great piece of opportunism by us.

After the gig the secretary had the diary out and immediately pencilled us in for more Sunday night gigs - one to be played every 6 weeks - for a whole year. It was like discovering gold dust. With the bookings done in advance it meant we could tie it in with gigs in Manchester, Newcastle and Leeds. If it clashed with a weekend date in Scotland it didn't matter - we could slip down to Englandshire in no time, meaning we wouldn't have to pay for digs, either. There was also the added bonus of the Gretna Transport Café which was open 24 hours.

Anyway, one night after a gig at The Hibernia, we packed up our gear and headed innocently onto the motorway as per usual. During one stage of the journey there is a mountain you have to clamber over. We didn't worry too much about weather forecasts in those days, however on this occasion it started to snow very heavily - and without warning. It got heavier and thicker as we moved along, and then we came to a valley where the road winds round and down and up the other side. I felt the wheels were losing traction and panic soon set in. I didn't want to get us all stuck way up in the mountains with no refuge even to pull over. So I shouted to the rest of the band to get outside and get on the back bumper to give us some more weight on the back wheels. In a flash they responded. We slipped and slid for a bit and eventually the wheels gripped allowing me to get some more speed up. I had to keep going now no matter what, refusing to stop until I got to an area of road where the wheels could grip the road more easily. Unfortunately the rest of the band was about a mile behind me. I certainly couldn't go back and pick them up. All of a sudden my panic about the road went to panic for the others. What if they all froze before they reached me, I worryingly pondered to myself?

It was snowing heavily, and halfway up a mountain the conditions were dangerously low. Then, in the midst of drifting snow I could just see flashing lights peering out of the gloom. A police patrol van had arrived on the scene. They positioned their van up against mine and motioned for me to wind down the windscreen. I explained to them what had happened, whereby they said they would drive the mile or so it was down the road and see to the rest of the band.

A few minutes later the police van came back up the hill. Thank God I said to myself. They've managed to find them OK. Wrong. There was no-one in the back of the van at all. They simply rolled down their window and said they were fine, and would catch up with me in a couple of minutes. I couldn't believe what I was hearing. I was livid. I started swearing at them. How could the police, of all people, leave them there like that? It was like Siberia out there. It was inhumane. Luckily another member of the band who stayed behind with me in the wagon stopped me from getting into bother. Never in all my days had I witnessed such disregard for fellow human beings. They could have been lying frozen in the snow – dead. Fortunately the lads did arrive, frozen, but in good health. I felt bad, especially as Joe – who had polio, and whose ankles meant he could not walk very fast – had been one of those who had to make the long trek up the hill. I'll never forgive the police for that.

Afterward I opted to take everyone to the Gretna Transport café and treat them to breakfast. It gave us a welcome chance to defrost. The next day I awoke to the sounds of the radio. The news reporter revealed that the road we struggled to get through the previous night had in fact been closed due to the amount of cars and trucks that got stuck in the snow. It was closed for three days.

This is me sat on my pride and joy - my first car, a Jaguar.

MARMALADE

The groupies giggled like the little teenage school girls they were, as Dean Ford arrogantly urinated off the back of the boat. It was sometime in the early '70s and the last night of our four-day tour with Scottish pop band Marmalade.

We were on our way to Dunoon - a small island off the south-west coast of Scotland - on a chartered ferry. We hadn't been paid for our previous three gigs, we had barely eaten more than three cheese and ham sandwiches between us all, and we were all sick to the back teeth watching so-called rock stars like Marmalade's singer act like an attention-seeking 10-year-old.

A typically twee pop band, Marmalade was managed by Peter Walsh, a pop entrepreneur whose portfolio included artists like the Bay City Rollers and The Troggs. Their only real success was a Top 10 cover of The Beatles' Ob-la-di Ob-la-da and received faint praise from Jimi Hendrix who liked their song, I See The Rain. They also recorded Hey Joe as a B-side, which was a hit song for Hendrix also.

Like The Viceroys, they toured extensively, their lust for alcohol on tour giving birth to their very own cocktail - the Marmaladdie. To me, the only interesting thing about Marmalade was they had two bass players in the band, which, though totally unheard of at the time, was nothing compared to some showbands who often had four sax players in their band.

What annoyed me the most about them though, was their inability to play more than a dozen songs, barely playing beyond a half-an-hour set. The Viceroys, however, didn't just play until the cows came home; they would usually play for another three hours after they had been locked up in the barn. It took us more than 30 minutes just to get our amplifiers warmed up.

Perhaps we were just cheesed off that we were skint and hungry. Or hung up because Marmalade was getting all the attention from the girls and we weren't.

After playing headline tours ourselves for so long, now it was us who were to be the support band. In those days, support bands were called "Relief" groups, which, back then, was a relatively new thing. It also meant you got treated like something you might step on in the street if you're weren't up to scratch. For instance, whilst on the tour with Marmalade we never got a proper soundcheck. We never got a rider either (a cup of tea and a few sandwiches was too much to ask for), and we never got the respect of the fans, who, as you might imagine, turned up purely just to see the headlining band.

Sitting on the boat watching Dean Ford make an idiot of himself while a light drizzle rained down on me, I pondered the question I'd asked myself so many times on tour with The Viceroys: How did it all come to this? Brian Wilson, that's how. Not to be mistaken with the famous Beach Boy, the future Member of Parliament, a student at Dundee University at the time, spent his summer months out with university term time promoting gigs before going on to found the West Highland Free Press and becoming a politician.

The Dunoon-born Wilson famously got Pink Floyd and Genesis to play Dundee Student Union for next to no money at all, a knack that continued when he eventually encountered The Viceroys. He'd heard us play before and thought we'd be the perfect support band for Marmalade. Despite having a Number 1 hit record in the charts at the time, Marmalade's gigs were pretty tame, so Wilson - who knew all too well we could make an audience get up on the good foot thanks to our ability to play really good swing music - got in touch.

When Wilson first called me up to book us on the tour, he was reluctant to tell me who we were going to be supporting; all he said was we'd be playing four dates with a famous group, outlining just how much The Viceroys would expect to earn from it, which wasn't a whole lot.

It wasn't until we turned up at The Corran Hall in Oban - where 50-to-60 screaming teenyboppers were standing outside waiting for the headline band to arrive - that we finally saw the name of the band we were supporting on a poster hanging in the foyer.

Ronnie, meanwhile, was outside talking to some of the girls when he spotted our new tour mates.

"Did you see those Heads, Jim?" said Ronnie, Heads being a reference for musos back in the old days. "Their hair is longer than some of those girls standing outside. Real greasy it is, too."

"They look like a hedge that's been dragged through a hedge backwards," Joe concurred, as the various members of Marmalade waltzed past us barely acknowledging our existence.

Just like the teenyboppers, we weren't allowed anywhere near the band. By the time we got to Campbeltown, I doubt Marmalade even knew there was a support act on tour with them, let alone knew who The Viceroys were.

That said, on the last night of our short tour we were asked to go back on stage after Marmalade had completed their set. Why? Because Marmalade had no more songs left to play. The audience wanted their money's worth, so, to satisfy the baying mob of pigtails we went back out and played for another half an hour.

Brian Wilson, meanwhile, who was always immaculately dressed, turned up to the show wearing a tuxedo and a dickey-bow. Everywhere we went he seemed to be deliberately avoiding us. I'd had enough experience as a manager to know that when a promoter is deliberately avoiding you it's probably not because you smell funny.

When I eventually did catch up with him to tackle the issue of money, he said to come see him after the gig. Fair enough. After I came off stage, I made a beeline to the production office to confront him. Unsurprisingly he'd bailed. Split. He'd counted up the night's takings and made a bolt for it halfway through our set.

For the next two months I constantly telephoned Wilson leaving messages on his answering machine asking him where our money was. I even wrote him threatening letters explaining what The Viceroys might do to him if he didn't cough up the cash. But it was fruitless: we would never see our money.

As I cursed his name in the dressing room after the gig, also backstage was one of Marmalade's "assistants" - one of those guys who seek out the best-looking girls for the band. You know, help find them drugs, chase up the best digs in town - a general dogsbody in other words. Well, this particular vagabond informed me, that, not only had Wilson bailed on us without paying us our money, he was about to set sail on the last ferry back to the mainland.

Without hesitation I put my running shoes on, and ran as fast as I could down to the ferry port. Blowing through my backside and having almost coughed up a lung, I arrived two minutes too late. As the ferry pulled out of the dock, I stood at the harbour mouth helpless, as Wilson - and all our money - sailed off into the Scottish sunset never to be seen again.

DUANE EDDY

The not-so-sweet Marmalade experience left a very bitter taste in our mouths. Thankfully, as the years rolled by not all the gigs we landed with famous bands or famous singers were as unpleasant to endure. Case in point: PJ Proby.

A Texan rocker, who came from a wealthy oil and banking background, Proby was a mountain of a man, a great, good-looking performer who looked and sounded like Elvis, and who appeared with The Beatles on their first big TV show - Around The Beatles. He had Top 10 hits with Hold Me and Somewhere, yet somewhat ironically failed to score a hit with a song John and Paul wrote for him entitled, That Means A Lot.

We found ourselves on the same bill as Proby during a sojourn to Redcar in Northumberland where American folk singer Tim Hardin - who wrote If I Were A Carpenter and Red Balloon - also appeared. It was a Sunday night gig, a regular concert where the audience sat down - no dancing or anything like that. Proby was amazing: he was larger than life. He came across like Elvis's dark twin: demonic, destructive, and hypnotically fascinating. He was dressed like a cowboy, all velvet trousers, ruffled pirate-style shirt and buckled shoes.

After slaying the audience in typical fashion, he trudged off the stage with the sort of swagger only the Pelvis himself could carry.

When we came to play, we only had enough time to play a forty-five minute set, so we made sure we played all our best songs. Fortunately we not only impressed the audience, we impressed the promoters and talent scouts, too, that were following Proby and Hardin around on their UK tour.

Backstage, The Viceroys chatted to Proby while I dealt with the promoters in an attempt to pick up more work. Negotiations were going well until the promoters asked me where we were based. Soon as I told them we lived in Scotland their shutters came down. Bang! The conversation was killed stone dead. No matter how good we were, because we weren't based in London, no-one was interested.

We also supported The Kinks at The Carlton in Slough, the home of ballroom dancing. As usual, we were kept well away from the headline band and forced to change in the toilet, which is where I believe the term "toilet tour" came from: not because the venues were toilets (sure, some of them were), but because you had to get changed in them. Changing into your suit while someone did a number two in the cubicle next to you isn't a heart-warming experience. Still, that was the sort of thing that can happen when you're leading the life of a struggling musician.

The Kinks, let it not be forgotten, were a great band, and it was fantastic to hear them play, even if hardly anyone did turn up to watch them. It was a midweek gig after all, so what could you expect? Back in those days, people rarely came out unless it was a weekend gig... no matter how famous the band was.

Indeed, when we got the chance to support Motown girl group, Martha and The Vandellas - who had hits with Dancing In The Street, Nowhere To Run and Jimmy Mack - it, too, was a quiet affair, as people stayed away in droves for midweek concerts. A brassy, gospel-influenced singing trio, Martha and The Vandellas sounded all the better thanks to their raw, very famous, soulful backing band, The Funk Brothers. We grew up listening to Motown and Stax soul, now we got a chance to hear it first hand.

Before the '70s ended, we even played on the same bill as Siouxsie and the Banshees, which proved The Viceroys came through skiffle, psychedelic rock, hard rock, glam and punk. There wasn't much gobbing going on at the gig, nor much in the way of violence, as was common of punk gigs at the time. I did have one issue with punk, though. I came from an era where knowing how to play your instrument was considered a valuable and commendable talent. During the days of punk such a thing was considered bourgeois. To Siouxsie's credit, though, she, and her band, came across as very polite and respectful. But then, they wouldn't want their audience to know that.

The Viceroys however, were also lucky enough to back Duane Eddy during a rare foray to the UK. The most famous and most successful instrumentalist of all time (in guitar terms), he had a unique, unmistakable echoing, twanging guitar sound that led him to become (according to the New Musical Express in 1960) World's Number One Musical Personality, ousting Elvis Presley from his long held position. Amazingly for us, The Viceroys were fortunate enough to share a dressing room with the big star at a gig at the highly prestigious venue that was The Bankies Football Supporters Club in, where else? Clydebank.

Now, Duane Eddy was one seriously big dude. Ronnie, our guitar player, on the other hand, was tiny - a shrimp at 5 foot 2 compared to Eddy. A few minutes before Duane Eddy was about to go onstage, I rushed back to our dressing room to tell the rest of the band Eddy was about to begin his set. When I got there I was met with hoots of laughter. Ronnie, standing in front of the dressing room mirror and looking like a small flagpole of leather had found Duane Eddy's pure leather and cowhide jacket. Naturally, he just had to try it on. Picture a pantomime cow with an Irish accent and you'll have some idea how silly Ronnie looked.

"Hey everyone," mumbled the little tyke from underneath a mountain of cowhide. "Do you reckon anyone would guess it was me if I went out in front of the audience and pretended to be Duane Eddy?"

Everyone let out another huge roar of laughter. Meanwhile, as we almost peed our pants howling at Ronnie, no-one happened to notice the towering, looming shadow of Texas guitar-slinger Duane Eddy - all 6 foot 4 of him - standing at the door, glaring at us like God on the Last Day.

Everyone fell silent in an instant. Some of us gazed at our feet, while others stared out the window hoping Eddy wouldn't notice them. Cool as you like, Eddy strutted across the room like a swaggering cowboy at high Noon, peering down at Ronnie whose little cowhide boots must have been quaking with fear. Eddy sized Ronnie up and down as though he were about to make a quick reach for an imaginary pistol from an imaginary gun-belt. He grabbed the collar of Ronnie's new-found coat, cupping his rather large left hand underneath Ronnie's chin. I felt a lump in my throat the size of a swollen turnip. Ronnie must have been feeling a rather larger lump in his pants.

"Erm, nice jacket you have there," Ronnie smirked. You could almost hear Ronnie's knees knocking. "Know where I can get one like this?"

Time stopped. Then, suddenly, Eddy let out a huge, booming laugh, slapping Ronnie over-generously on the back. Everyone spontaneously cracked up with laughter. Phew. What a relief. For a minute there I thought Eddy was going to rip our heads off, as well as Ronnie's entire body, for taking the piss out of him. Instead, Eddy just lit up a cigarette, poured himself a drink, and pulled up a chair before inviting us all to gather round him as he recalled the story of Leon Atkins - a blues guitarist, who, just like Ronnie had jokingly intended to do a few minutes earlier, got his break into showbusiness by impersonating another musician.

Huddled round the gigantic star, as Eddy regaled his story about Atkins, we all felt like cub scouts sat round the campfire roasting marshmallows. In reality, we were a bunch of paddies in brown suits sat around a rickety coffee table listening to one of the biggest guitar greats of all time wax lyrical about a blues guitarist no-one had ever heard of.

His name? Leon Atkins, an 18-year-old guitarist, who, in 1958, was playing small juke-joints when an opportunist moment changed his life forever. A favourite of the locals and others who heard him play, one night in an upper scale blues club a well known blues artist by the name of Jimmy Reed was scheduled to perform. Leon knew Jimmy Reed's music really well. Having grown up listening to jukebox music from the nearby night-club, it had always been Atkins's hope to see Jimmy Reed perform live.

Reed, however, turned up at the club inebriated, leglessly drunk and unable to perform. Atkins, who everyone knew could play Reed's parts blindfolded, was quickly summoned to take his place as they sneaked Jimmy Reed out the back door. As no-one really knew what Reed looked like, the crowd couldn't tell the difference and the show was a hit. Atkins gave a show stopping performance, and thus he was reborn as Lil' Jimmy Reed before going on to develop his own style of blues-guitar playing.

As Eddy finished his story and got up from his chair, we all got the feeling his story was his way of teaching us a lesson; that while fate certainly has a hand in deciding who becomes famous and who doesn't, the real road to success was to be yourself. And with that, the Texan cowboy swished out of the room with the august grace of a revered cardinal.

It was quite a tale, and probably one of the most bizarre events to happen to us as a band. I mean imagine that: The Viceroys impersonating another band to grab all the glory? As if.

The Viceroys: This is a photograph taken from a flyer we used to hand out at gigs. That's me standing at the back holding my trusty trombone. Notice Ronnie on the far left holding his guitar, Jim Delaney below him with the saxophone, and Brendan, our one-time singer above him.

NESS SURPRISE

With the '70s now in full swing, The Viceroys started booking gigs through a Glasgow agency that another band, The Fontanas, were also part of. The Fontanas - not to be mistaken with Wayne Fontana's band - had been with the agency since it was founded and were therefore the agency's "pet" band. This meant they got all the best gigs going. To be fair, though, The Fontanas had done a lot of spade work for the agency: well known in most towns and cities, they even had their own LP out through the budget K-Tel Records, which cost about 20 shillings or so to buy. Affordable, you could say making a record through K-Tel was the old-fashioned method of burning your songs on to a CD. The bonus was major retailers and music shops were willing to stock them for you, too.

One weekend The Fontanas were booked to play a Friday and Saturday night at the Caledonia Hotel in Inverness. The director of the agency, however, realised he could earn them, and himself, twice as much money by pitching them up at a big farmers' convention in Cumbria. So, as we had no gig ourselves that weekend, we got sent to Inverness instead. Trick was no-one told us we were replacing The Fontanas.

It wasn't until we arrived at our guest house in Arconnell Street, beside the castle, in Inverness, that we discovered our name hadn't been advertised in the paper. Unbeknownst to us, the press deadline had passed, the agency director too lazy to bother making the necessary advert changes in time. The landlord, a fine chap who was always quick to give us an extra rasher of bacon for breakfast, and who always made sure we received the morning paper, always kept an eye on the papers to see who was playing in town on the weekend.

"Sorry, lads, I just can't see your name in the paper. They must have made a mistake or something."

"A mistake?" I cried. "I'll say there's a mistake. Without any advertising, we'll be lucky to get one man and his dog along to the gig."

Later on, down at the hotel, we introduced ourselves as "the Irish showband who had been booked to play."

It was only 3pm (we always arrived at gigs early), so after setting up our gear, a couple of the lads decided to go downtown for a quick pint, have a couple of games of pool perhaps, and maybe do a wee spot of shopping.

At the local Woolworths store, Ronnie and Brendan discovered a long queue snaking its way halfway down Academy Street. Curious, the lads took a closer look.

"Hello. What's going on?" said Brendan, using his enquiry as an excuse to chat up one of the local girls.

"Everyone's buying The Fontanas' LP," said one of the girls. "You know - the Irish showband? They're playing the Caley Hotel tonight and tomorrow."

Immediately Ronnie and Brendan turned on their heels and rushed back at to the guest-house Godspeed where I was having forty winks.

"Jimmy! Jimmy! You'll never guess what!" I could hear them shouting as they both ran up the stairs before charging into my room.

"Calm down, guys. Can a man not get five minutes kip before a gig? What's the problem? Is one of the band drunk?"

"No, it's nothing like that," Brendan panted. "It's worse. The Fontanas. There was a huge queue of teenagers lining up to buy the new Fontanas LP from Woolies."

"Are you meaning to tell me you ran all this way to wake me up to tell me that?" I mumbled back. "So what?"

"No, Jimmy," Ronnie butted in. "The Fontanas: the teenagers were buying their LP because it's *them* who are meant to be playing at the Caley Hotel this weekend - not us."

I paused for a moment to let this information sink in. Then the penny dropped.

"I knew it. The director of the agency - he's swapped us with The Fontanas without telling us. That's why our names are not in the paper," I moaned, frantically looking around for the local paper.

Sure enough; in the Entertainments section of the local newspaper was The Fontanas' name advertising their gig at the Caley. I couldn't believe it. I got on the phone to the agency right away, but, as expected, the director was nowhere to be seen. What were we going to do now? We were due onstage in a couple of hours, and half of Inverness' teenagers were going to turn up expecting to see The Fontanas instead.

By now the rest of the band had arrived back at the guest-house, and as we sat in the residents' lounge trying to figure how to get ourselves out of another fine mess it finally came to me.

"To hell with it all, lads, let's just pretend we are The Fontanas this weekend," I begged the band. "Who's going to know we aren't them?"

"Jimmy, you're off your head," said Joe. "No-one's going to buy that. Soon as one of them clicks we're not The Fontanas everyone in the auditorium, including the staff, will know they've been duped. Then what? Eruption. People will storm out. Our reputation will be in tatters."

I wasn't to be out done. We'd just travelled ten hours from the south west of Scotland to be here. Now I would be damned if I was going to let the agency director's arrogance ruin our reputation and screw us out of a weekend's worth of gigs.

"OK," said Ronnie. "Let's say we do pretend to be The Fontanas. There's another problem - we hardly play any of the stuff that The Fontanas do. They play a lot of Irish folk - we hardly play any of that."

Ronnie was right. Granted, we could play some Irish folk, but compared to The Fontanas - who could play Irish folk music more convincingly than us - it was a bit like saying you could box just because you owned a pair of boxing gloves.

"Right, listen up," I said. "Let's do a little bit of detective thinking here. There's a good chance not everyone in the audience has bought The Fontanas' album. The photograph on the front sleeve isn't that clear anyway, and it's not as if they're hugely famous. I mean, how many teenagers in Inverness really know what they look like? If we keep the lights down real low no-one will be able to see us clearly, even if someone does know what The Fontanas do look like. And in any case, the teenagers here like to dance. They're not going to spend the entire gig looking at the band now, are they?"

I knew I was kidding myself, but an executive decision had to be made. Do we come clean, apologise for someone else's mistake and drive another ten hours back down the motorway with no wages in our pocket? Or do we take a professional risk and play the gigs anyway? It was settled.

"Come on, then, guys," I said to the others. "It's Friday night... we've got a gig to play."

WE, THE FONTANAS

I was leaning on the side of the wagon behind the Caledonian Hotel in Inverness. How we had got away with it I couldn't really tell. A few teenagers who had attended the Saturday night gig smiled curiously at me as they walked past me on their way home. I smiled back at them nervously, hoping they wouldn't see what was painted across the back of the wagon. Then the rest of the guys spilt out of the tradesman entrance, got into the wagon, and sped off making our getaway. None of us stopped to look behind us.

By some bizarre miracle, we had just managed to play two nights at the Caley Hotel without anyone (including the hotel staff) realising we were not The Fontanas.

On the Friday night The Fontanas' fans wasted no time in coming up to the stage with song requests from The Fontanas' new LP. The LP had 12 songs on it, of which we only knew 2 the whole way through. This was a major problem. In my mind I was sure we would be lynched, denounced as impostors, tied to a cross and run out of town on a rail. I'd got the band out of a tight scrape before, but not even Houdini could have escaped from this one.

Two minutes into the gig, though, and the first request: "Can you play The Wild Colonial Boy?" it said on the wee bit of paper tossed up on to the stage. The band all looked at each other as if to say "Sorry, no idea."

"Me neither, Jimmy," Brendan whispered in my ear.

We knew little bits of the song, but none of us knew all the words to the entire tune. So, to get by, Joe and I took turns at singing the verses we did know, even if it did mean singing slightly out of key with one another. Luckily no-one seemed to notice, but surely it was only a matter of time before we were rumbled.

Minutes later, a young couple came up with another request. As the band played on, I bent down and spoke to them direct:

"Look, I'm awfully sorry but the lead guitar player sings that song. He's got laryngitis at the moment so he won't be able to sing it. I can sing Bold O' Donoghue and the Seven Drunken Nights - how about that? It's the best we can do I'm afraid."

Fortunately, they just smiled, said it wasn't a problem, and continued dancing. How many times was I going to have to deliver that spiel before the night was out I wondered?

Reassuringly, the audience was having a great time and paid little or no attention to us. The lights were so dim it was like being surrounded by thick fog, and we were so far back from the audience we all looked like we were in soft focus.

When someone did ask for Irish folk music, we gave them a dose of The Dubliners or some Clancy Brothers - stuff The Fontanas regularly included in their set. What worried us then, however, was whether we would get paid or not. The management at the hotel didn't know our true identity after all. Had they discovered we were impostors they would surely point to the fact the contract had not been accurately fulfilled, before dumping us out on the street without a penny in our pockets, our reputation and ability to play this fair town again in ruins. So the idea was to stay out of their way as much as possible.

The following night - Saturday - we managed to pull off the same trick. Keep the lights down low, stay out of the hotel staff's way, and pretend that all song requests were originally sung by our poor lead guitarist, who had mysteriously and unexpectedly come down with a nasty case of laryngitis. Miraculously it worked.

After the gig was over, we picked up "our" pay cheque before making a swift getaway in the wagon. As I put the last of our gear away, some kids from the dance took a short cut to the bus stop via the small lane we were parked in at the back of the hotel. About a dozen of them stopped to say hello, some of them looking at me with suspicious eyes as I draped a huge sheet over the van's back doors. Had they seen "The Viceroys'" name emblazoned across the back in big letters, the cat would have surely been let out of the bag.

Talk about the luck o' the Irish.

Sligo: Yeats Country, where I spent many a lazy summer visiting my grandparents.

MARATHON

You don't get much sleep when you're in a full-time working band. And if you happen to be the manager of an Irish showband called The Viceroys, then you get no sleep whatsoever. Take the time we played what I refer to as The Marathon for example.

We were booked to play a student ball in St Andrews as part of a bigger bill that included two recording groups, a Dixieland band, a jive band, a blues band, and a showband (us). With a gig to play in London the next day we were hoping to get the earliest slot on the bill before making a quick exit and getting on the motorway. No such luck. We were given the last spot, which meant playing from 2.15am to 3.00am - a five-hour wait before getting the chance to play.

If we had hung around and drank booze we'd have been too drunk to perform, drink too much coffee on the other hand, and we'd have been wired to the moon. So we petted our lip, drank soft drinks, and tried to enjoy the other bands.

By the time we were due to play, we were all heading for the land of nod. It wasn't the stage manager waving us on stage, it was Mr. Sandman holding a big, warm-looking sleeping bag.

No sooner had we finished our set and slunk all our gear into the back of the van, it was practically daylight. The birds were singing, and love-bird students - walking hand in hand and kissing each other - were making their way to the beach to continue their respective romantic shenanigans. I turned the key in the ignition and looked out at the road before me. When would I get to sleep next I wondered? We had to drive over 500miles. How many hours was that? 10? 12? Who knows? Whatever, we headed on down across the Forth Bridge and onto the A1, passed Leeds, and were making good time before slipping onto the M1.

To pass the time, Ronnie had come up with a humorous way of keeping us all amused. Every time we stopped at traffic lights, or at a service station, he'd make this comical "fffit" sound every time he pointed at a pretty girl in a dress. A cross between the mime of Harpo Marx and the Stooge-esque antics of Eric Morecambe, this quickly transcended into "fffit-ing" at everything by everyone. It certainly beat playing I Spy that was for sure.

With the time passing by nicely thanks to Ronnie's comedic magic, we were now only about an hour-and-a-half outside London, and not too far from a place called Wovern Sands, which has brickworks with about 15 chimneys. As we drove passed it, smoke started billowing from our own chimney, in this case, our engine - it had blown.

Black smoke mixed with oil spewed onto the windshield obscuring my vision, causing me to weave across the road like a maniac. I wound down the side door window, popped my head out and tried to rub it off with a beer coaster, whilst trying not to drive into oncoming traffic at 75mph. But it was no use; the wagon had finally packed in, so we pulled over at the side of motorway.

It was 4pm now and we'd been making great time, well on target for our Monday night gig, and with plenty time to get to our digs, get fed, get washed and all the rest of it. As usual though, everyone turned to me for the answers. The answer was we were stuck on the motorway, with no phone in sight, and no-way of getting to our gig in time. This was calamity. We had to phone the agent.

I walked a mile to the nearest service station when a police van spotted me and kindly picked me up before driving me the rest of the way to the station. Surprisingly, the agent was cool about the whole ordeal, saying he would send a van out for us right away to take us to London. We might not be able to check into a guest-house and change our clothes, but maybe, just maybe, we'd get to the show in time.

When I eventually got back to our wagon I was hoping our new transport would have arrived. Sadly, no. Two hours passed and there was still no sign of the replacement van. Apparently it had been driving up and down the M1 looking for us, although how it never spotted a huge wagon smeared in oil, and with The Viceroys' name slapped across it in big colourful letters I'll never know.

Anyway, I hitched a lift back to the service station and the phone booth, whereby the agent informed me about the van combing the motorway looking for us. Luckily the driver met me a mile down from the service station. We dumped all our stuff into the back of our rescue van and ventured on our merry way to the Big Smoke, Godspeed. By the time we arrived at our destination it was 7.30pm, all of us looking like zombie North Sea Oil workers who'd just been raised from the dead. As we slithered wearily into the hall the venue manager came out and stopped us in our tracks before we could unload any of our gear.

"Just what exactly is it you are doing?" he snapped, looking at us as though we were lazy builders who'd just stumbled upon the Savoy for a quick lunch.

I told him who we were.

"We were informed this afternoon that you had broken down on the motorway and unable to play the show," the venue manager continued, "so we went ahead and booked another band to take your place instead."

Now, in the '70s, showbands travelled a lot. If a showband failed to turn up for a concert - say they broke down like us on the motorway, fell ill or had some other genuine excuse - the venue, more often than not, would have a resident band available that they could phone up and come fill the slot. Fair enough you might think. But, considering we had endured a long, long road trip, hadn't slept in what felt like two days, had run the risk of being mowed down walking 10 miles along the motorway (me, of course), and witnessed my beloved wagon blow its engine. Well, no way was a resident band going to take our place now.

Seething? I was the Guns of the Naverone. A mushroom cloud. High Voltage TNT. We could have throttled the guy. Instead, we simply turned on our heel and marched quickly back out the door, got in the minibus and found the nearest phone. The agent again.

Refusing to panic, the agent said we could go over to a club in the Harleston district and do a spot there. We were originally penned in to do a spot later that evening anyway, so the fact we could do a double-header in the one venue certainly helped relieve some of the stress we'd endured. Yet when we arrived there was but another drama to attend to. The Binson Echo Chamber. The crème de la crème of vocal amplification – our dear Binson was gone. Vanished. There was six people singing in the band, and harmonies were a big part of our act. The echo chamber enhanced your voice like no other PA system mixer could. Pink Floyd was its biggest advocators and the Binson bestowed an aesthetic value that has many collectors bidding silly money for on eBay today. The most precious item within our arsenal, without it we would be nothing.

Ronnie, however, assured me he had definitely carried it into the venue with him. The hall inside the venue, though, was virtually pitch-black, and we couldn't find the stage lights. So once we set up the remainder of our gear, we pulled out every trick in the book to try and stall the start of the show while Ronnie put his miner's hat on and went looking for the echo chamber.

Backstage, meanwhile, we only had water and hand towels to wash ourselves with. We didn't have any time to have a shower, and there were still traces of oil on our suits after the gig: another expensive trip to the dry cleaners.

I hadn't slept in 48 hours and no amount of grooming could disguise it, either. 45 minutes after we were due to go on, Ronnie finally arrived back at our dressing room carrying the Binson Echo Chamber under his arm like he was carrying a flask of tea to work. Thank Christ for that. Apparently he had left it on the floor at the back of the hall, in the darkness. My feet were also killing me. The fatigue was setting in and I thought I was going to pass out, but alas, the show had to go on.

Finally onstage, we broke into our usual glut of pop party-rousers. Suddenly a whole bunch of glamorous girls arrived - about 20 of them in tight mini skirts, legs up to their dangly earrings, hair as big as the state of Texas. These were the same girls who used to come and watch us back in Ireland before they moved to London in one big group. They'd settled in well to London life; however I think they, too, were led to believe its streets were paved with gold. Even so, Ronnie often wrote to these girls and it was nice to see some familiar faces at the gig.

At the end of the night, at about 3.15am, we were totally fagged out, though still awake enough to talk to the girls, naturally. Of course, we nagged them with our tales of woe - then reality hit us. We had nowhere to sleep. We didn't even have the wagon to kip in. The girls said they didn't live too far away - a 15-minute walk to Willesden - and invited us back.

"Just come and stay with us," they said. "You'll have to sleep on the floor, though. If the landlord knows we have boys staying - we'll get chucked out. So be quiet."

So off we went back to the girls' gaff.

The girls all lived in a single-sex flat; it was taboo to have mixed-sex flats in those days so we had to save their embarrassment, and possible eviction, by creeping out early in the morning. I slept on the hard floor, using my jacket as a pillow and a couch throw as a blanket. It wasn't quite a four-poster bed with soft, puffy pillows and a goose-feather mattress, but it was better than sleeping out on the streets of London, which I might add, are paved with chewing gum, fag ends and dog dirt. I think I managed about two hours sleep.

Stuck in London for the week, we had no wagon to get around in, so our London promoter said he would find us four or five nights work in some North London venues. Luckily he found us a driver to take us from gig to gig. Next problem: Digs. In the morning, I made my way to a guest-house in Highbury, just along from the Arsenal football ground and not far from the girls' flat we'd stayed the night previous.

We were under no illusion we all looked terrible, like rag and bone men on the look-out for cheap bric-a-brac. Indeed, the landlady looked at us aghast. I told her our sob story, and she did feel some pity for us despite her initial suspicion. I reasoned with her, telling her we'd give her a deposit there-and-then before paying her the rest of the cash later in the week. Much to our relief, she took us in.

On our first day at the guest-house, there was about a million pants and socks hanging out to dry, so with no washing machine available to us, we all had to hand wash them in a basin (yuck!). Not for the faint hearted, after we'd scrubbed our undies thoroughly it was time to go down town and buy come new clobber with the money we'd received for last night's gig.

We didn't pull in the sort of cash that could buy us tailored suits from West Saville Row, but in October there were plenty of stores in an area just up from Finsbury Park selling out-of-season summer fashions that could be picked up for next to nothing. I bought myself a nice overcoat for the oncoming winter, but when I got back to the guest-house, Brendan was there to meet me, wearing the exact same jacket - same colour and everything! He'd popped into the same store as me about five minutes after I had. What were the chances of that?

Sadly, those jackets bring back sad memories. One Sunday, back in Ireland, we set off to play a marquee dance in a place called Duleek, which, for all you music anoraks out there, is where Oasis' Liam and Noel Gallagher's granny comes from. Getting there meant travelling along a very narrow road, and as we approached the junction that takes you off the main road, we came up behind a small car, an Escort, I think. As it pulled out from the junction, another car slammed right into it side on. The people inside the Escort didn't stand a chance.

Brendan and I got out the wagon to tend to the injured, but there was nothing we could do. The young couple inside the Escort died almost instantly on impact. They just sat there, like someone had just turned off the lights. So Brendan and I took off both our matching overcoats and placed them over the unfortunate couple. The other two people from the other car who had crashed into them emerged unscathed. We found a phone-box to call the relative authorities, before heading off to the gig under a dark cloud.

Traditionally, those who booked us for gigs in rural places lay on (what in Ireland is called) a ham tea. The little old lady who welcomed us at the marquee took us into her cottage and cooked us up a mighty feast fit for the King of rock and roll. We drank our tea, but although we hadn't eaten anything all day - and wouldn't be able to eat again until another four hours later - the upsetting experience we'd just witnessed earlier left us devoid of any appetite. We were ill. Not sick as in vomiting, but nauseous nonetheless. The trauma of seeing those poor young people die right before our eyes left a dark mark on us that was to be everlasting.

Anyway, I digress.

Back in London, I phoned our agent in Scotland one evening to give him an update on what had been happening. Our wagon was in bad nick to say the least. It was going to take six weeks for the engine to be rebuilt - a lifetime in the world of a travelling band - so I got on the phone to the local social club back in Newton Stewart. The Viceroys had a good arrangement with the social club, so they offered us their minibus to get around in. It kept us on the road, and ensured we honoured all the gigs we'd booked while our wagon was being repaired in London.

The plan, now, was to get back to Dumfries, then take the train down to London once the wagon was fixed and come back to Scotland with it. So, with a couple of nights left until we took the train back north, we sat around twiddling our thumbs hoping our London agent would phone us up with news of a gig.

Being a Monday night, there wasn't much hope. Then, as luck would have it, the 'old dog and bone' started to ring and we found ourselves high-tailing it down to an Irish club for another gig. Result.

The punters there tried to cajole us into playing rebel songs for them, though not the bigoted ones some are so-called today. These songs were sad, historic laments. Older rebel songs were mainly protest songs disguised as love songs so as to not offend the English who were ruling the Irish at the time. Take My Dark Rosaleen for example. Rosaleen, in this song's sense, represents Ireland - a metaphor for the country and the dark times it suffered under English rule. A lot of songs were like that because the country was ruled by an English King. So the rebel songs were a more subtle way of passing on information.

Marty Ford, the wonderfully brilliant classical singer I've already talked about, was singing for us at the time, and what a show he put on that night. An inspirational performer who oozed class and sophistication, he could do all the Roy Orbison songs, and could melt the hardest of hearts. However, like all geniuses, he had his problems.

Next day, though, we were back on the train and heading home. It was good to be getting home. Our week-long London stint had been pretty stressful. London was a strange place to put it mildly. Promoters didn't want to know you unless you were based there. What you normally paid in rent for a month in Scotland barely saw you through a week in the Big Smoke. Getting anywhere was a logistical nightmare (no satellite navigation in those days, boys and girls), and making friends wasn't too easy either, as people are always coming and going in London.

We no longer had a wagon, either. We relied on others for help, some of our musical equipment had gone missing, and we had to scrub our own dirty pants.

Coming home, we all felt insecure. We'd hit rock bottom. Frank, who owned the holiday park we used to stay in, turned up in his landrover. He had a trailer attached to it so he could transport us, and our gear, back to Creetown in. Oh my God, this really was bad. I had done so much unselfish work on the band's behalf the rest of The Viceroys let me ride with Frank so I could travel home in relative comfort while they rode in the horse cart.

The marathon was over, but unlike most marathon runners I didn't feel like we had achieved anything. In some ways, coming back to Scotland felt like crossing the finishing line last to no fanfare.

THE 2i's

I had rarely seen a Jenson Interceptor let alone been inside one. It was the mid-'70s and Cliff Richard's manager was giving me a spin around London in a car you were more likely to see in a James Bond movie than in real life.

24 hours earlier, one of his business associates was walking down Old Compton Street in Soho dressed in a long trenchcoat, smoking a big fat cigar. He looked like Orson Welles on his way to a porn theatre. We were playing a gig in Soho that evening, a couple of the guys had gone uptown to the music shops, so I ventured down to the venue to unload some of the less heavy equipment (the guitars and brass instruments) when he nudged up alongside me.

"Excuse me, guv'. In a band, are ya?" he said, pointing at The Viceroys' colourful logo on the side of the wagon.

At first I thought he was pointing to our Irish license plate: The Troubles in Northern Ireland were well known and I had a notion he was from Special Branch or MI5, and about to give me a serious grilling for being Irish and unloading mysterious boxes in downtown London.

"Aye - we're a showband," I replied nonchalantly, hoping this potential undercover policeman would buzz off as quickly as he arrived.

"Really? How convenient," he snorted, taking out a tin of snuff from his Inspector Clouseau-style foot-length coat and inserting it up into his nostrils. "What sort of stuff do you play?"

My back was killing me lugging all the gear out of the wagon. Soundcheck was fast approaching and none of the guys had stayed behind to help me. In other words, I was in no mood for small talk.

"Oh, you know," I said in a tone of voice only a man with a big trombone case strapped to his back could muster. "Folk, country, rock and roll - all the hits from the Top 40, too. We're onstage at 8pm if you want to come hear us? Anyway I don't wish to sound rude but I really must be getti..."

"Oh, I do apologise," he said cutting me off. "I didn't mean to get in your way. I just thought you might want some extra work. Sorry to bother you."

He turned on his heel and strutted off down the street at pace. I dropped Ronnie's guitar case with a large thunk.

"Work?!" I shouted after him. "Erm, what kind of work do you mean? Sir?"

He walked up to me casually and outstretched his hand.

"Hello, Paddy," he said. "My name's Paul - Paul Lincoln."

The next day, myself and the rest of The Viceroys turned up outside a dark, grotty-looking coffee-bar cafe on the opposite side of the street where Paul and I had met 48 hours previous. From the outside there was certainly nothing imposing about the cafe. It was the kind of place hundreds of people would walk by without even giving it a second glance. The frontage consisted of a large pane of plate glass, to the right of which was a glass door with a chromium handle. Someone had pasted a 7-Up (a popular lemonade soft drink) sign on the door, either as an inducement to purchase or perhaps to prevent the inattentive from walking headlong into it. An oblong sign hung above the window and door. It said: "The 2i's Coffee Bar - Home of the Stars." What kind of a pretentious name is that for a coffee bar I thought. None of us had any idea how famous this place actually was.

In 1958, The 2i's was the fuse for the explosion that was to come in the world of rock and roll. It was a melting pot for musicians. Adam Faith, Hank Marvin,

Tommy Steele - they were all discovered here; they even hung out here when they weren't playing in the basement bar. Cliff Richard's career began within the walls of The 2i's as well, and it was partly down to Paul Lincoln, who, like Led Zeppelin's manager Peter Grant, was a wrestler and wrestling promoter before he got into music and bought the place. The place had soul, a magnificent buzz about it.

Inside, we trudged through the glass door past the jukebox and walked straight ahead between the serving counter and the coffee machine. At the end of the room we marched down a narrow stairway that led down to one of the world's most famous basements in live music, perhaps only second to The Cavern in Liverpool. A battered old piano sat on the stage. The place was so small you could have fitted it in a matchbox. It was tiny. You'd be lucky if you could fit 40 people in there, let alone a band on the stage.

"Was this stage built by John West?" said Ronnie making a caustic yet witty remark in reference to the famous brand of sardines. "We'll have to set-up on the floor."

Sam, sporting an American-style crew cut and white James Dean-style T-shirt kept effing and blinding as he battled in an attempt to set-up his drums without toppling everyone else. In turn, Ronnie, wearing a mustard-coloured suit and holding tightly onto his thirty-quid electric guitar, kept bumping into Joe who had Brylcreemed his hair like some 1930s movie idol for the occasion.

Brendan, never one to keep his mouth shut, turned to me and said: "All this hassle for three lousy songs, Jim? What's the craic, here, eh?"

The three lousy songs we played turned out to be our audition to join the same management agency as Cliff Richard's. After we'd finished playing, Paul Lincoln invited me up into his office - a cramped wee broom cupboard basically - and pushed a contract to conduct a three-month tour of Germany under my nose. He handed me a pen, a cheap biro. I picked it up and stared down at the paper. My writing hand began to shake a little.

"Go ahead," said Paul urging me to do so. "Sign on the dotted line and you'll be on your way to Germany. That's where The Beatles made their name, you know."

It was like being back in Bonici's office in Elgin when he offered us six months in France.

Back at the digs in Tottenham Court Road, we sat down and went over the pros and (mostly) cons of going to

Germany. I'd asked Paul if we could have a couple of days to think it over. No problem he said, take all the time you need.

We'd been reading horror stories about bands getting ripped off by shady agencies and promoters promising the kind of success The Beatles were supposed to have (yet never) encountered during their stint in Hamburg. In fact, that Sunday I'd read a disturbing story in the Sunday Mirror about a female singer who had a horrific time in Germany. She was never paid for any gigs she played (the promoters wouldn't give her any), she had no place to change before her shows (sometimes not even a female toilet to change in), and, more often than not, left with nowhere to stay. We knew other bands had similar problems, too, in terms of not getting paid, and being stranded in a strange land tied to a contract you couldn't get out of. Well, it was a big decision to make.

We had no midweek gig the following week so I took a walk back down to the 2i's to see Paul. He was busy on the phone when I arrived, so I stood about admiring all the famous people on the posters that adorned Lincoln's office while he, as Elvis would say, took care of business. I even let myself imagine that one of the people on the posters was me and my band.

"Come on, kid!" Paul shouted, slamming the phone down and grabbing his dodgy looking trenchcoat from the coat rail. "I've got loads to do today - you can talk to me in the car while I run a few errands."

Outside The 2i's was Paul's pal and associate, Jonny Foster, who was also Cliff Richard's manager at the time, sitting in a Jenson Interceptor. One of the first steel-shelled cars ever produced, it was also one of the first manufacturers to equip a production car with four-wheel drive and came with antilock brakes and traction control. It also made the driver look like he was in The Saint, which was one of the most popular TV shows at the time.

Zooming around London in Foster's flashy piece of kit, Paul came straight to the point as we skidded around the corners of Soho attracting stares wherever we went.

"Look Jimmy," he said puffing on a cigar. "You've got a great band there. You're tight, well-rehearsed, you have a good pop sound - perfect for the agency. Are you in?"

I was still in shock from his initial offer a few days previous. The offer was certainly tempting: sign with Cliff Richard's management and go to Germany, just like The Beatles.

At the time, Cliff Richard was huge. We'd have been on the same roster as him. But then, the risks. Oh yes, the risks. We weren't a well-known or successful band, but we were professional lads who had their heads about them (most of the time anyway), and we'd come too far to have it all blow up in our faces. So I took a big breath, more of a sigh actually, and 'fessed up to Foster.

Paul didn't say very much as Foster drove us back to The 2i's, and where I'd left the wagon. To his credit, he didn't try to get me to renege on my decision to turn down the contract to Germany.

As Foster sped off in his luxurious mobile, Paul simply shook my hand and wished me all the best before disappearing inside the place where British rock and roll first came alive. Part of me felt I was doing the right thing, while another part of me felt like I'd just shook hands on another missed opportunity. Germany, like France, and, soon, America, weren't about to receive a visit from The Viceroys anytime soon.

Almost 40 years on from The Viceroys' audition at The 2i's, the famous venue is today called the Boulevard Bar and Dining Room. A Green Plaque sits at the site to commemorate its existence. The basement where we played those three short songs, and one of the most famous stages in the world, is now a lobby area. The interiors and names may have changed, but the memories, needless to say, will always remain.

Drogheda: A typical postcard of my spiritual home in the Republic of Ireland, and also the town where The Viceroys were founded.

ALBERT HALL BLUES

How Jesus managed to fast in the desert for 40 days and evade the Devil's temptations dwelled on my mind. It was Lent and I was driving the wagon to a nearby Wimpy bar driven by the temptation of a burger and some chips. I hadn't eaten anything in 40 hours, now I was ready to drive forty hundred miles if it meant getting to stuff my face with something satisfyingly savoury. Had Wimpy been around in Biblical times, Christ would definitely have succumbed to Lucifer. To coin a popular phrase and guitarist's name, I was Hank Marvin.

Satisfied after scoffing down half a cow, washed down with a side order of guilt, when I got back to the parked wagon, I discovered a card with a hand-written message placed under one of the wagon's windscreen wipers. It was from one of Bernard Delfont's producers.

Now Delfont was part of Britain's most famed entertainment dynasty, a theatrical impresario and producer of movies such as The Deer Hunter and the Jazz Singer. Bernie staged the Royal Variety Performance and reinvented the London revue with the massively successful Talk of the Town. Why his producer had come down to see us play during our week-long stint in the Tottenham district was unclear to me. He said he represented Delfont, so I agreed to speak to him after the gig, where he asked me if I, and the rest of The Viceroys, wanted to play a charitable gig Delfont was organising to be held at the Royal Albert Hall. The Royal Albert Hall? Yeah, right. I thought he was putting me on, thanked him for watching our show and said nothing more about it.

The message he left on the wagon's windscreen said: "Dear Viceroys, I wasn't kidding when I asked if you would like to play at our annual fund-raising gig to be held at the Royal Albert Hall. Please get in touch as soon as possible. The concert is to be held on the last Saturday of this month. Here's our number. Thanks."

I put the card in my trouser pocket and ventured back to the digs with it to show the rest of the band.

"The Royal Albert Hall!?" spluttered Ronnie, almost choking on his cornflakes (breakfast usually started at lunchtime for The Viceroys). "You've got to be kidding me, Jimmy."

I pulled out the band's diary.

"Sorry, boys. We've got a gig on in Preston that night so we won't be able to play the Royal Albert Hall."

I said it sarcastically, as though I were joking. I suspected one of the lads must have written the note themselves and placed it under the windscreen wiper before I got out my bed that morning. The band was forever pulling tricks on each other to pass the time, and anyhow, we were a largely unheard of showband from Ireland. Who would want us to play at the Royal Albert Hall? Get real.

The band all looked at me as only a puppy-dog can. Not only were they adamant they weren't up to any tomfoolery, they really, really wanted to play the gig. You could see it in their eyes: The Viceroys' name in neon lights, TV cameras everywhere. Fame at last, recognition, a recording contract. I quashed their hopes as fast as their eyes lit up. Someone was having a laugh. We would never cancel or pull out of a pre-booked show, whether it was the annual Drogheda school fete or Shea Stadium. I was 100% confident it was a wind-up. If I'd turned up at Delfont's offices asking about a gig at the Royal Albert Hall I'd have been kicked halfway down the King's Road. We were going to Preston to play that gig and that was the end of it.

A few months later I bumped into Delfont's so-called producer again in an Irish club in London's east-end. He asked me why I never got back in touch with him.

"Well, to be honest, we couldn't play the last Saturday in September because we had a gig already booked," I told him, which, true as it was, also offered up a plausible, if crazy alibi.

He looked at me with a mixture of puzzlement and disdain.

"What?" he said, shaking his head in disbelief.

"I wrote 'next' month on the card, as in October? Not 'this' month as in September. Jimmy, the offer was kosher, am sorry to say."

Embarrassed, and with a sudden weakening feeling in my knees, I thanked him for the initial offer, but pretended I wasn't all that bothered before making my excuses and leaving the bar. I had barely taken a sip from my pint. Oops.

TIMES A' CHANGIN'

As the late '70s saw the emergence of punk, bookings began to cool off as the band soldiered on from one gig to the next. I had become increasingly frustrated with the way the band was functioning. The job wasn't as fun as it used to be, and what used to come relatively easy was now a frustrating slog. Our fees were beginning to drop, too, forcing us to take on more work just to make ends meet. And with some band members now in their mid-30s, people were re-examining their priorities.

Worse, Ronnie, one of our longest-serving members, had decided to leave. His girlfriend, who wanted to get married, have a family and settle down, was constantly nagging him to spend more time in their new house together and less time on the road with the band. I understood his predicament: we were no longer 20-somethings without a care in the world. The band, like so many others, had been something of a rite of passage for Ronnie. We shook hands, wished each other the best, and parted on good terms.

Without Ronnie in the band, we now needed a guitarist - a guitarist who could also sing comfortably, too. It didn't take long to find a suitable guitar player, but unfortunately he couldn't sing a note.

Then I discovered a great vocalist who couldn't play rhythm guitar. Nuts. We were a showband, not an orchestra. Taking on two members to compensate for one was, literally, taxing. So we spent less time gigging, and even less time rehearsing. The time we did spend together, as a band, was very little to say the least. Then there was our long, long, long overdue trip back to Dundee.

The last time we played there we performed at the Caird Hall to 2000 teenagers who queued up afterward to collect our autographs. Now we returned to a scuzzy, wee cabaret bar buried somewhere in darkest Dundee - a section of town taxi drivers don't like to drive through. There were more holes in the walls than a pound of Swiss cheese, and it looked as though people used the tiny stage we were expected to fit upon for peeing against. It certainly smelled like it. There was an older crowd in - we were more used to playing to audiences in their late teens and early twenties - and the (very) few who stayed to watch us play barely looked up from their pint glasses to acknowledge us. As I stood out looking at the empty barstools through the fug of tobacco smoke, I couldn't help think back to that great time we had at the Caird Hall. Back then, it had been all so different.

Then we got ripped off on a trip to Darlington, which is not too far away from Newcastle. We had been offered £2000 for a week's work, a week's worth of gigs that started at midnight and featured very, very little in the way of an audience. A typically nondescript club other than it had a bar built from pennies and engraved with copper, it was obvious the club owners weren't making any money and we didn't get a bean at the end of it. The club hadn't paid the agency our fee, so the agency, obviously, couldn't pay us. The agency we were dealing with - who were based in Manchester - said they couldn't help us directly, and offered no other support other than advising us to take it up with the club. It was a depressing embarrassment.

I couldn't tell the boys, and as I was paying them a salary, I had to pay them while yours truly walked away with nothing. The rest of the band probably thought I was making a fortune, but it was me who had to absorb the losses and keep the band running.

With the band struggling physically and financially, I was forced to make an all too rare appearance behind the drum kit.

We were due to support Pickkety Witch - a British bubblegum group fronted by Polly Brown, and who had hits such as That Same Old Feeling, Sad Old Kinda Movie, and Baby I Won't Let You Down - when our regular drummer decided he couldn't make our Middlesborough gig. It was one thing to support such a big act; it was another thing to follow them. Talk about a tough act to follow.

I hadn't played drums since my days in the Crilley School Of Music band, and the only time I played drums during my time with The Viceroys was during our rehearsal tea break. What was I going to do? No-one else in the band could play drums, and it wasn't like us to cancel a show on account of having no drummer. As they say, the show must go on.

To add insult to injury, when we arrived at the venue I discovered that the stage conveniently harboured a drum-riser that sat almost two meters above everyone else, putting me in full, glorious view of the audience. I couldn't escape. Mistakes were going to be made, no question about that. So there was only one thing to do - pretend I was back in the Crilley School of Music band where you just smiled, looked like you were enjoying yourself, and tried not to show any signs of perspiration on your brow in a feeble attempt to convince the paying public you knew what you were doing.

Fortunately for me - and everybody else for that matter - the audience wanted music by The Dubliners and the Clancy Brothers, which meant the drum-beats were easier to play. No intricate drumming skills or fancy paradiddles required, thank God.

With mistakes kept to a heart-comforting minimum, the gig sauntered past reasonably well with no obvious hiccups. Like the time I injured my hand playing with the Crilley School of Music, I'd managed to blag it. Just. Yet what surprised me the most was how tame the audience was. Here, they appeared to be contented, foot-tapping types who enjoyed Irish music and country and western.

In Leeds, the previous night, we had been met by coin-throwing Led Zeppelin enthusiasts. Nevertheless, while we had narrowly got away with this one, the cracks within the band were now all apparent for everyone to see. Our saxophonist - another exceptional talent also called Jim - packed his suitcase one morning after a gig, leaving without so much as saying good-bye to anyone. The next thing I heard he was playing in Las Vegas for almost £2000 a week.

Joe, meanwhile, had been offered a steady job in Glasgow, playing country and western at a residency in Shawlands. For him, it meant he no longer had to travel more than 5 miles to a gig. His polio was getting worse, and the thought of being confined to a cramped van journeying 500 miles up and down the country understandably no longer held much appeal for him. I could hardly argue with him. Joe had been a great servant for the band - again, another one of the longest-serving members in the group - and I was too disenchanted myself to try and talk him out of it.

The band had spent a lot of years together. Now we had pretty much all left the flock, moving on to other adventures in life. As the band dwindled, I found myself being offered a lot of music agency work. I'd built up a lot of contacts organising all the band's gigs, and the comfort of a warm office and a steady wage appealed.

I organised tours, scheduled boat trips, bus journeys and train bookings for travelling showbands, set up hotel accommodation around the country, and yes, located spare guitar strings at ungodly hours. It was just the same as running the band, only I didn't run up the mileage on the wagon, stayed in the same warm bed every night, and didn't have to worry about eating something that was brown and lumpy. Then the possibility of a trip to America came a' calling.

Equity laws in the UK at the time insisted that no British act or musician could perform in America unless three American acts appeared in the UK. Tit for tat basically. Our old friends, The Fontanas, meanwhile, had been paving the way for Irish showbands to get over there, heading out to the ski resort of Brodie Mountain in Massachusetts, which some people will know, was John F. Kennedy country. Other American acts came over as part of the deal, and the whole thing kind of mushroomed from there. The Americans loved The Fontanas, especially the ethnic aspect. They loved Kennedy which meant they loved the Irish, so they could do no wrong.

Meanwhile, an agent in America I was in contact with kept assuring me that The Viceroys could come out there and do coast-to-coast tours lasting six months. There was even talk of getting on the Ed Carson and Ed Sullivan's shows. It was hard to believe it was a possibility.

The director of the agency, meanwhile, was belittling me a lot. He would come in to the office after we'd set up bands in the towns and venues they were due to play in and swap them all around without a care in the world. Arrogant to say the least, he was undermining the work I was putting in - and the trust instilled in me by the bands and venues I was liaising with. I'd organise and pay for newspaper adverts and he'd swap the gigs as he saw fit. It was expensive, and while he could walk out the door without a worry, it was me who would get all the flak. It was upsetting and we nearly came to blows over it.

Meantime, The Fontanas were breaking ice in the States. While they were helping make a name for themselves, and creating possible opportunities for Irish showbands over there, it also meant they weren't playing in the UK, thus allowing us to take up a lot of their (well-paid) gigs.

Even more inspiring was Brendon Boyer and the Royal. They were now playing in Las Vegas and sharing a billing with Elvis Presley. They were on a 5-year contract; they wanted more money and landed another 5-year stint after that. There's every possibility they're still playing in Las Vegas today.

The agency were good to me, though, despite the agency director's incessant interference. I was given accommodation, well paid for my work despite the director's carry-on, and I had a lot of influence around the office, on staff workers and bands alike. I kept in touch with the agent who was taking Irish showbands over to America, so it was only a matter of time before The Viceroys got the invite, and the chance to re-energise ourselves.

The director, too, was aware of what was going on in America, and it wasn't long before he got himself involved. He wanted to jet out to New York and meet with the agent, sort of arrive in a whirlwind and pretend he was "the man". The director just had to be in control. He couldn't let it go. But the only thing the director succeeded in doing was stepping on the toes of the agent. He undermined what the guy was trying to do for the Irish showbands and cut him out of negotiations. The result? No more bands from our agency going out to America. It stopped The Viceroys from making any possible waves in America, which would have renewed our enthusiasm, motivated us, and got the band back on track. Not that I'm bitter or anything, you understand.

Later on, some members of The Viceroys got married and started families. We hadn't learned any new songs in months, and discos were now all the rage. Bookings were drying up. Live music was being given the heave-ho. Suddenly, promoters were booking DJs because they took up less space and cost half the price of a band.

"It's what the kids are after" promoters would tell me.

The Viceroys, however, continued to plug on and play the occasional gig. We were fading. It wasn't that playing was no longer fun, it just wasn't exciting. We were maturing, too. We'd been on the road for a long, long time, and the things that were fun when you're 21-years-old aren't the same when you're 35. Did we really want to be pushing 40 and doing the same thing?

Myself, and the rest of the band who were in the last incarnation of The Viceroys, still can't remember how things finally came to an end. But did it? I wouldn't say it came to a dead stop, but if anyone in the last line-up of the band can remember when we played our last gig, then no-one is any the wiser.

Yet despite all the ups and the many downs, the biggest highlight of the band's life came to us by pure chance. It was at a gig in London and our biggest-paying gig ever. We'd been invited to play at the Grosvenor Hotel on St. Patrick's Day, always a celebration, from the White House down to the local village hall. We were staying in Tottenham, between the Arsenal and Spurs football grounds, at the time and loaded with the flu.

Luckily, though, we'd been offered to play a dinner-dance, which required little effort even when choked with the flu.

We arrived at the tradesman's entrance at the back of the hotel, hoisted our gear out and into the ballroom. Our eyes almost popped out their sockets. All around us were these beautifully round ornate tables, all tastefully laid out for the guests, a bottle of every known alcoholic drink laid out in the middle of the table. What a temptation. We could have helped ourselves to ten bottles of whisky or brandy or gin and they would never be missed. We didn't succumb; however, we just needed to get on with setting up for the show.

As the hoity toity ate and drank and smoked, we stood far away in the corner playing away quietly. Some got up to dance, which certainly helped the gig go by quicker, all the ladies in the house looking strikingly beautiful, resplendent in their long, elegant-looking gowns. Real class.

After an hour or so, we were told to take a break and given the chance to sit down with everyone else and have something to eat and drink. No sooner had our backsides touched the chair, up went the skirl of Irish pipes. A piper came down the hallway's long, flowing staircase followed by the guest of honour - wait for it - the Irish President.

We couldn't believe it. We were playing a gig all right – for the President!

Of all the mishaps and bad luck stories that followed The Viceroys, this one almost made up for all of them. We might have endured some hardships and tragedies along the way, but it didn't get any better than playing for the President of your own country.

A WORD FROM THE MANAGER

I still have a problem thinking of the band in the past tense. I committed a substantial chunk of my life to my little-known Irish showband. Suffered the tragedies that came our way, and endured the heartache of coming so close to achieving a little slice of fame and success. Yet, as the years have passed I never fully came to terms with the reality that there would be no more tours, no more gigs, no more driving the wagon up countryside hills and down single-track roads. Nevertheless, I always sensed we hadn't heard the last of The Viceroys. I'd always harboured the notion of documenting my time in the band, but never seriously.

That all changed when my son showed me a photograph of The Viceroys he'd found on the Internet back on Easter Sunday, 2007. The first thing I did was figure out what had happened to all the band members after the band split up. I'd hardly seen anyone since the band faded away. During the band's career about 20 different people played in The Viceroys, ranging from those who played one-off gigs, to those who stayed in the band for several years. It wasn't easy remembering all the names.

The ones I could remember still lived in Drogheda; others remained behind in Scotland after the band faded away, while a couple of others moved to America and Canada. The majority of us though, got married, settled down with kids and got good jobs.

Joe Gilchrist, who played bass, and the only member of The Viceroys to keep in constant contact with me after the band stopped playing, was the longest serving member of the band, after me. I first met him at the train station in Manchester after he had answered an advert I had placed looking for a new bass player in an Irish newspaper.

The first thing I noticed about Joe was that he had polio, though he never let it hinder him, in real life or on the stage. The next thing I noticed was that he smoked a pipe (and still does to this day). Joe had played with a lot of showbands, and was a little older than the rest of us, so we held him in great respect. He was my right-hand man in a way, and when The Viceroys stopped, he joined another band offered a contract to play in America. The band was a seven-piece, and as only six of them were allowed to go, poor Joe got the chop. He stayed with his sister in Dublin for a while after that until he got back on his feet, and up until a few short months ago continued to make a living from music, this time playing in a country band in Glasgow.

For the others in the band, I imagine The Viceroys, for them, was a bit of light relief, something to look forward to at the end of the week. For Joe, however, it was his life, and it affected him the most if others weren't too bothered about getting regular gigs. He was a great bass player, and he still comes down to see me for a cup of tea and a chat.

Ronnie, as far as I know, still lives in the south-east of Scotland, and a very contented chap. He's hard to track down, but I hope to meet him again.

Sam, one of our longest-serving drummers, used to play in the brass and reed band and was chuffed to bits to be playing for us. Like the others however, he was under the thumb and gave into pressure from his girlfriend to quit the group.

Our best-ever singer, Brendan, still lives in Drogheda. Still a dry wit with something to say about everything, he hasn't ruled out another dramatic return to the stage.

Myself? Well, as the band faded into the background, it took a while for me to regain my equilibrium. After all, The Viceroys was my baby. After all the years I'd spent with the band, it was difficult to think of starting anew. I didn't sing, pick up the trombone or play the accordion again for months. At one point, I wondered if I ever would again. So I did some soul-searching and took some time out.

Agency work paid my way for a good while and I continued on with my life, moving to Glasgow, getting married and seeing my two wonderful children (Kevin, who is now an engineer, and Sarah who would carry on the Watters family musical tradition and become a drummer and a piano player) come into the world.

Later on, I took to working on my daughter's stall at the Glasgow Barrowland Market every Saturday and Sunday, selling everything from laundry detergent to soft drinks. The craic is always good, and it gives me the rest of the week to spend time with my children. And, for being a supposedly old fuddy-duddy, am actually quite up-to-date with some modern music - Guns 'n' Roses being one of my favourite bands.

I support live music by going to lots of gigs - the Celtic Connections festival in Glasgow is a must-see every January - and I still own a record player, complete with Lesley speakers (which older readers may know, is a large wooden cabinet driven by a rotating horn.).

Sadly, however, my teeth have softened with age, meaning I can no longer play the trombone. You need to purse your lips in a particular way to play it, so if I attempted to blow into it now I'd only end up doing my teeth and gums damage. These days my music-performing exploits go no further than singing a few tunes in the shower. Whenever I'm feeling nostalgic, though - usually after a couple of Sherries - I'll put on an Elvis or Eddie Cochran record and take out the trombone from behind the cupboard, take a look at it and think of all the great gigs I played with it in The Viceroys. I do miss my band.

Ironically, The Viceroys are, today, more famous now than they ever were in the '60s and '70s. Type the words "Viceroys Showband" into Google on the Internet and you'll see a few photographs of the band (there are many sites dedicated to Irish showbands), plus messages on music messageboards from people who were either in the band, or came to see us play. It amazes me that millions upon millions of people around the world can find out about The Viceroys, years and years after we spent so long driving thousands of miles in the hope a few people might remember our name.

When I look back now and think of all the showbands there were, what pleases me the most is how stylish we all looked in our dapper suits, how varied we all were in what we could play (no genre was taboo), the hanging around after gigs signing autographs, handing out photographs, cavorting with all the girls who would follow us - sometimes across different countries - just to hang out with the band. What made showbands sound so great was their great rhythm sections, incredible brass and strong vocal harmonies. Sadly, what killed all the showbands off was the introduction of Disco. Popular, cheaper to book, why pay out money to six or seven or eight musicians, when you only needed one man to operate a record deck? Those who loved the showbands weren't even given a choice, as dancehall owners concentrated on profits.

To people like me, the age of the showband is well and truly gone. But music goes in cycles, and I've no doubt well-dressed men in tailored suits, backed by Brasso-cleaned trombones and driving brightly-coloured vans with their name painted on the side, will come around again. Thankfully there are people in their fifties and sixties who haven't lost their fervour for showbands. Some of those bands we played with are still on the go. There are even kids, not much older than my daughter, who are just beginning to find out about showbands and how they touched so many peoples' lives at a time when life was simpler, less hectic than it is today.

Simply put, there were no excesses. People didn't come to gigs to cop off; they came to get off on the music. Apart from the wacky-baccy, drugs weren't really a problem, either, and people back then could really dance. Just see the kids of today try to do the Hucklebuck, or the Madison. They'd be stiff as boards for a week.

Looking back, though, I have no real regrets. Of course, we narrowly missed out on TV exposure, slipped up on an opportunity to play the Royal Albert Hall, nearly entered America, and scupper tours in Europe - but we were professionals who always got on with the job.

"Where's the next gig, Jimmy?" I can almost hear Ronnie saying even now.

But unlike other, more famous bands who experience the excesses of rock and roll and split up after a couple of years, The Viceroys had a real sense of camaraderie and the laughs never really dried up. I would like to think that anyone who ever played with The Viceroys (short or long-term) would agree with me. The tragedies, the mishaps, the misadventures - all that befell us were largely out of our control.

As a band we never really made recordings - we never had the money or the opportunity. I still possess a tape-reel recording of a rehearsal we did, although the echo on the recording makes us sound like we'd recorded it in the Grand Canyon and not inside the village hall it actually took place. Nevertheless, it's something to hold on to, a physical and audio reminder that The Viceroys wasn't a dream or just a distant memory.

As I write this, there's even talk of getting some former members of The Viceroys back together for a reunion. If it happens, we might just get round to making a proper recording - over forty years after I first formed the band. It's quite a thought.

Back in the day, we never really thought the band would one day come to an end - it had been a way of life to so many of us. And now that the prospect of getting back together looks quite possible, I suppose it never really ended at all.

So, next time you hear of a showband arriving in your town, check the papers and the posters. You never know - it just might be The Viceroys.

THE END?